3D
STORYTELLING

3D
STORYTELLING

HOW STEREOSCOPIC 3D WORKS
AND HOW TO USE IT

By
Bruce Block
&
Philip Captain 3D McNally

Focal Press
Taylor & Francis Group

NEW YORK AND LONDON

First published 2013
by Focal Press
70 Blanchard Rd Suite 402
Burlington, MA 01803

Simultaneously published in the UK
by Focal Press
2 Park Square, Milton Park, Abingdon, Oxon OX14
4RN

Focal Press is an imprint of the Taylor & Francis Group,
an informa business

Notices
Knowledge and best practice in this field are
constantly changing. As new research and experience
broaden our understanding, changes in research
methods, professional practices, or medical treatment
may become necessary.

Practitioners and researchers must always rely on
their own experience and knowledge in evaluating
and using any information, methods, compounds,
or experiments described herein. In using such
information or methods they should be mindful of
their own safety and the safety of others, including
parties for whom they have a professional
responsibility.

Product or corporate names may be trademarks
or registered trademarks, and are used only for
identification and explanation without intent to
infringe.

Library of Congress Cataloging in Publication Data
Block, Bruce A.
3-D story telling : how stereoscopic 3-D works and
how to use it / by Bruce Block & Philip Captain 3D
McNally.
pages cm
1. Digital cinematography. 2. 3-D films. 3.
Photography, Stereoscopic. 4. Computer animation.
I. McNally, Philip. II. Title. III. Title: Three dimensional
story telling.
TR860.B56 2013
777'.6--dc23
2012040461

ISBN: 978-0-240-81875-7 (pbk)
ISBN: 978-0-240-81876-4 (ebk)

Typeset in Avenir
By Joanne Blank

CONTENTS

3

CHAPTER THREE - *The Six Visual Sins*   **59**

4

CHAPTER FOUR - *3D Aesthetics*   **113**

Appendices   **188**

FOREWORD

In December, 2004, I walked into an IMAX theatre for a screening of *Polar Express*, curious to see how the film used the new technology of motion capture. But I walked out blown away by the film's use of an old technology – stereovision, aka 3D.

Until this movie, 3D was noteworthy mostly for being featured in a few 1950s' horror movies. Well, the real horror of these movies was that they often induced headaches and nausea due to the fuzzy, poorly sync'd analog images. In *Polar Express*, digital technology had completely solved these problems. The 3D imagery was crisp and vivid and, most importantly, it enhanced the story.

Nevertheless, after the film was over, my head still ached … not from eyestrain, but from the realization that I had just seen the future and DreamWorks Animation was now going to have to undertake a massive retooling to become a 3D production studio.

In order to achieve this transformation, one of the smartest moves we made was to hire Phil McNally, who we all got to know as Captain 3D. There is no one on the planet who better understands, or has more passion for, 3D storytelling. With Phil's help, we became the first studio in the world to produce 100 percent of its films in 3D.

This move to 3D has been incredibly exciting. I imagine that our experience is similar to what occurred at movies studios in the 1920s and '30s when the technologies of sound and color arrived on the scene. These were extraordinary developments that greatly expanded the filmmaking vocabulary. So, too, 3D.

For me, personally, it has been a tremendous pleasure to work with Phil. And now anyone can learn from him thanks to this book. Phil and the equally expert Bruce Block have written a true bible on 3D as a storytelling medium. This book is invaluable for filmmakers, and it should also be fascinating for filmgoers. Millions of people around the world have witnessed how 3D dissolves the flat plane of the movie screen, converting it into an open window that allows us to not just watch movies but truly dive into them. This book offers a chance to dive even deeper, in order to gain a full understanding of the multitude of creative choices that bring about so much amazing imagery.

So, put on your 3D glasses. You are about to enjoy a whole new dimension in the art of filmmaking.

Jeffrey Katzenberg
Chief Executive Officer
DreamWorks Animation

ACKNOWLEDGMENTS

The authors would like to thank Ray Zone, Sean Phillips, Dave Drzewiecki and Matthew Low for their suggestions and help during the development of this manuscript. Ray passed away unexpectedly as this book went to print. His love and passion for 3D has inspired us all and he will be missed.

Thanks also to Dreamworks Animation for supporting 3D in their feature film production.

A special thank you to Suzanne Dizon.

If you have comments or questions about this book, you may contact the authors at:
3Dbooknotes@gmail.com

The 3D images in the book can also be viewed online at
www.focalpress.com/cw/block

INTRODUCTION

Photo courtesy of Pinsky/Starkman Collection

Stereoscopic 3D photography has been around since about 1840. Originally, it referred to the optical illusion of depth in still photographs. Early stereoscopes, like the one pictured above from 1859, displayed two nearly identical photographs, one seen only by the left eye and one seen only by the right eye. The observer would look through the two lenses and their brain would combine the two photos into a single image that appeared to have three-dimensional depth.

The first stereoscopic feature length film, *The Power of Love*, was shown in 1922. But stereoscopic movies remained nothing more than a novelty. In the 1950s, stereoscopic 3D features like *House of Wax* and *Bwana Devil* created a 3D movie fad that only lasted about three years. Another revival attempt was made in the early 1980s but 3D remained on the fringes of major film production.

The digital age has made reliable stereoscopic 3D photography and display possible on large theatre screens, consumer televisions, and computers. This technical revolution has led to a renaissance in stereoscopic 3D production.

The term "3D" was originally coined in the early 1950s. Audiences learned that 3D movies meant putting on special glasses and watching a stereoscopic movie on the big screen.

In the late 1970s, Hollywood began using computers in feature film production. CGI (Computer Generated Imaging) or CG (Computer Graphics) were used to create visual effects and as an alternative to hand-drawn animation. These computer-based images were, unfortunately, called "3D" because they were created in a computer's virtual three-dimensional environment. Suddenly, the term 3D had two completely different meanings.

Today, the term 3D still refers to computer-generated visual effects, CG animation, and stereoscopic pictures. In this book, 3D refers only to stereoscopic 3D.

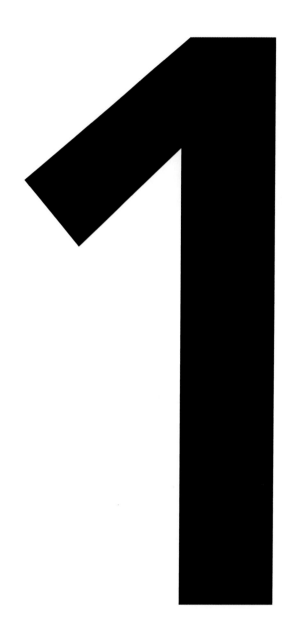

CHAPTER ONE
The Basics

Thinking in 3D

Stereoscopic digital cinema and television offer unique visual opportunities for storytelling but they also require picture-makers to rethink established filmmaking ideas. The screen is no longer a flat surface displaying a two-dimensional picture. In 3D, the audience is unaware of the screen and it becomes a window suspended within a three-dimensional space. Objects can now appear in front of the window and behind it.

3D is an amplifier for depth. When the staging, composition, and production design constructively exploit 3D, the visual world of three-dimensional depth opens up to the filmmaker and the audience.

3D has its own "visual language." Before you can speak the language, you must learn a new "visual alphabet." If you only know part of that alphabet, your ability to create 3D will be limited. Don't be impatient. It's not only about learning a new vocabulary, it's also letting go of some old habits that could keep you from fully understanding and using the 3D grammar.

Like any art form that depends on technology and craftsmanship, there are certain terms and concepts that must be understood. 3D is no different. Once you see and understand the visual possibilities that 3D offers, you can merge them with a story to produce an interesting and unique visual experience.

The first two chapters of this book explain 3D's technical and aesthetic variables. The third chapter deals with the visual problems and advantages that 3D presents to directors, cinematographers, and designers. The fourth chapter shows you how to use these variables and advantages to tell a story in 3D.

Human Vision and 3D Photography

To explain stereoscopic 3D photography, it's important to understand how people see in normal, everyday life. As we look around at home, at work, while playing sports etc., we see the world in three-dimensions.

In the real world, we see objects with <u>two</u> eyes. Our eyes look at or **converge** on an object. The term vergence is sometimes used for convergence.

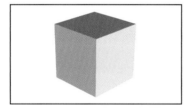

Left eye view

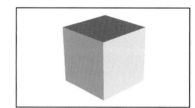

Right eye view

Because our eyes are about 2.5 inches (63.5 mm) apart, each eye sees a slightly different view of the world. Our brain combines or **fuses** these two views into a single three-dimensional image.

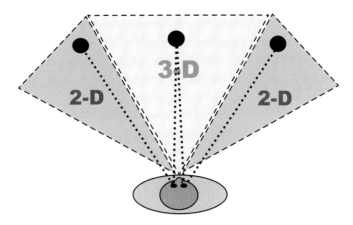

We only have stereoscopic 3D vision in the center area of our visual field. The left and right sides of our vision are only mono. This happens because the nose blocks one eye from seeing objects on the sides of our visual field. The left eye can't see objects on the far right and the right eye can't see objects on the far left.

Stereoscopic 3D photography replaces our two eyes with two camera lenses. This creates a photographic situation that has certain similarities to our own vision system.

Interoccular Eyes and Interaxial Lenses

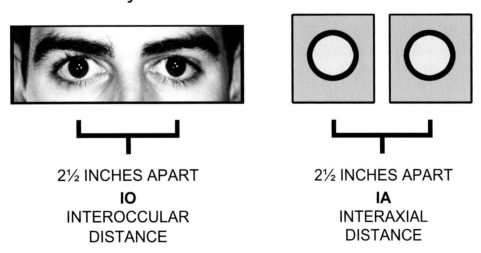

Human eyes (in adults and children) are about 2.5 inches (63.5 mm) apart. This distance or offset between our eyes is called the **interoccular distance** (or **IO**). The interoccular distance can be duplicated with two camera lenses and is called the **interaxial distance** (or **IA**).

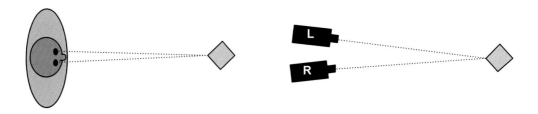

Like our eyes, two cameras converge on an object. Each camera photographs a slightly different view of an object.

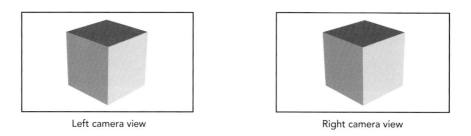

Left camera view   Right camera view

The two photographic views are called a ***stereoscopic pair.***

Stereoscopic 3D Camera Systems

There are two basic camera systems for stereoscopic 3D photography.

I. TOE-IN CAMERA SYSTEM

This illustration shows an overhead view looking down. The ***Toe-In*** system uses two side-by-side cameras angled inward.

Like human vision, each camera lens sees a slightly different view of an object. The two views create a stereoscopic pair. The orange lines at the back of the cameras indicate the position of the image sensors inside the cameras. The Toe-In system is primarily used in live-action photography.

II. PARALLEL CAMERA SYSTEM

This illustration shows an overhead view looking down. This camera system is called **Horizontal Image Translation** or **HIT**. Two cameras are placed side-by-side and parallel to each other. The orange lines at the back of the cameras indicate the position of the image sensors, which can be centered or offset. In the above illustration, the image sensors are offset (to capture the slightly oblique image in the frame). A variation on the HIT system offsets the lenses instead of the image sensor. The HIT system is primarily used in computer-generated (CG) animation, however more live-action productions have adopted it. HIT is also used in postproduction to adjust or correct the 3D image.

In the Toe-In or HIT system, the cameras may be combined into a single housing so there appears to be only one camera with two lenses. There are also some hybrid camera systems that combine aspects of the Toe-In and HIT systems.

Camera/Mirror Arrangements

This is not a third system, but an example of an alternate camera arrangement that can be used for Toe-In or HIT systems. The close positioning of two lenses side-by-side for stereoscopic 3D photography can be impossible because the cameras are too large. Mirror arrangements eliminate positioning problems and permit the cameras to be placed as optically close together as necessary.

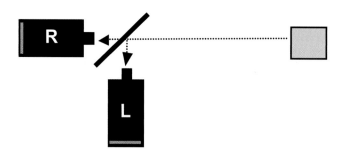

The above illustration is a side view. The two cameras are arranged above or below each other on opposite sides of a partially silvered mirror called a beam splitter. One camera sees through the beam splitter and the other camera sees an image reflected off the beam splitter's surface. The two cameras can be aligned on any optical axis without getting in each other's way and maintain a Toe-In or HIT relationship.

This camera arrangement is sometimes called under/through (or under/over). Depending on the 3D system and rig manufacturer, the assignment of left and right camera positions may be switched. For some circumstances, the cameras can even be mounted at right angles to each other in a side-by-side manner.

3D Viewing

In order to see 3D, the audience must view a stereoscopic pair of images. The stereoscopic pair of images must be separated so that one image is seen only by the right eye and the other image is seen only by the left eye. The stereoscopic pair of images from the eyes is combined or fused by the brain into a single 3D picture.

 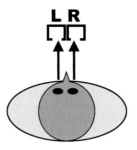 

Historically, most 3D pictures could only be seen by one audience member at a time. The antique stereoscope and the View Master toy are designed for a single user. Each eye is shown a completely separate image, which the single user fuses into a 3D picture.

As of the writing of this book, the best way for multiple viewers and large audiences to watch 3D is to use 3D glasses that separate the left and right eye images. There are several types of stereoscopic 3D glasses.

I. PASSIVE POLARIZED GLASSES. This system uses the technical characteristics of light polarization to separate the stereoscopic pair so that the viewer's left and right eyes see separate images.

II. ACTIVE SHUTTER GLASSES. These glasses have electronic liquid crystal shutters built into each lens, which are electronically synchronized to the 3D projector or television screen. As the screen rapidly alternates between the left and right eye images, the shutters alternate, allowing each eye to see the appropriate image.

III. COLOR FILTRATION GLASSES. These glasses modify the color of the left and right eye images. One lens is usually a red color and the other a blue color. These two colored lenses are optical filters that separate the stereoscopic pair of images for the left and right eye. These glasses come in various complexities but the simplest version is the cardboard anaglyph glasses used to view 3D comic books, magazines, and this book.

IV. AUTO-STEREOSCOPIC VIEWING. It is possible to see 3D without glasses. Lenticular or barrier screen technology can separate the stereoscopic pair for a small group of people and single viewer situations. Currently, these screens have viewing angle limitations but are used successfully on consumer televisions, computers, handheld devices, and camera viewfinders. Some systems for glasses-free viewing can track the viewer's position in front of the screen and continuously align the 3D for optimum viewing.

3D Projection and Display

A 3D movie projection system must display a stereoscopic pair of images, one image exclusively for the left eye and another image exclusively for the right eye. Here are two common projection systems:

I. TWO SEPARATE LENSES. One lens projects the left eye image and the second lens projects the right eye image. Both images appear on the screen simultaneously. The source of the two images can be two separate projectors or a single projector.

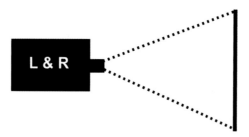

II. ONE LENS. 3D can be projected using a single digital 3D projector with one lens. The left and right eye images are typically projected alternately. The alternation is so fast that the audience thinks the two images are simultaneous. Future technology may allow simultaneous left and right eye projection through a single lens. Television screens can display left and right eye images alternately or simultaneously.

CHAPTER TWO
The Visual Variables

Orthographic Stereo

Seeing stereoscopic 3D pictures or movies is not really like seeing in real life. But, if you were going to create a stereoscopic 3D picture that comes closest to duplicating human vision you would arrange an ***orthostereoscopic situation*** and take an ***orthographic stereoscopic*** photo. "Orthographic" comes from the Greek words "ortho" meaning correct and "graphic" meaning visual presentation. An orthographic photo is created when all of the viewing conditions of real-life vision are duplicated in a 3D photograph.

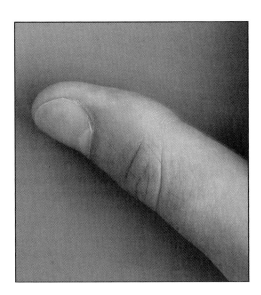
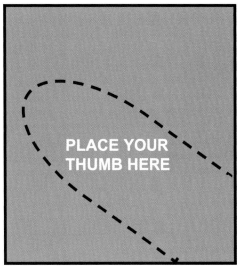

PLACE YOUR
THUMB HERE

Put on your 3D glasses, set this book 18 inches (46 cm) from your face, and place your thumb in the empty box. Look at the general size and three-dimensional characteristics of your thumb. Now, look at the orthographic 3D photo of the thumb in the box. That orthographic photo was taken with all of the characteristics needed to duplicate a real-life view of a real thumb. The orthographic photo of the thumb will appear as three-dimensional and lifelike as your real thumb (color, style, age, gender, manicure, and hairiness of thumb may vary!). If photographed and viewed under precise conditions, an orthographic photo can duplicate the human viewing situation.

Orthographic 3D photography has an extremely specific set of technical parameters. In order to take an orthographic photo, the stereoscopic 3D camera must duplicate four important aspects of the real-life view. These include:

1. IO and IA. The human eyes' interoccular and the 3D camera lenses' interaxial distances must match.

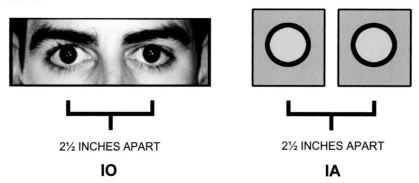

<table>
<tr><td>2½ INCHES APART</td><td>2½ INCHES APART</td></tr>
<tr><td>IO</td><td>IA</td></tr>
</table>

The IO (interoccular) distance between human eyes is 2.5 inches so the camera lenses must be set at a 2.5 inch IA (interaxial) distance.

2. FIELD OF VIEW. The human eyes' field-of-view and the 3D camera system's field-of-view must match.

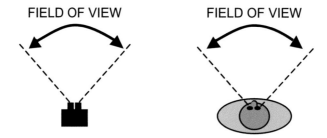

The exact camera image sensor and lens focal length needed to match the human field-of-view will vary depending on the camera system.

3. CAMERA DISTANCE. The distance between the viewer and the real object must be duplicated by the 3D camera and the real object being photographed.

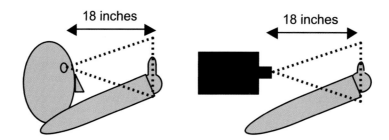

The viewer is 18 inches away from the real thumb so the 3D camera must be placed 18 inches away from the real thumb.

4. VIEWING DISTANCE. The viewer must be the same distance from the real object and the displayed orthographic image.

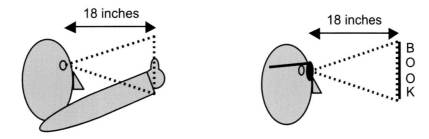

The viewer was 18 inches away from the real thumb so the viewer must be 18 inches away from the orthographic photograph of the thumb printed in the book.

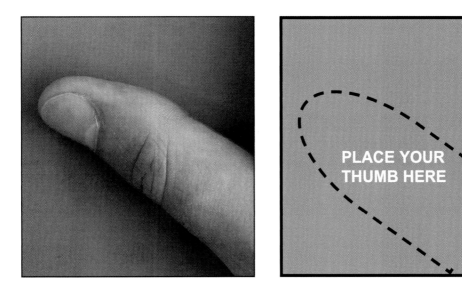

If the orthographic photo and the viewing situation are correct, you will have the identical visual experience as if you were actually 18 inches away from the real thumb. The thumb looks its normal size, normal shape, and has the same three-dimensional quality that it has in real life when viewed from the same distance. A 3D orthographic photograph comes as close as possible to duplicating a real-life viewing situation.

Using the same technique, an orthographic movie can duplicate the three-dimensional experience of watching a live stage show.

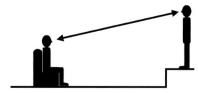

This orthographic movie will replicate the visual experience of one audience member sitting in the first row center watching a live performance.

A 3D camera is placed in the first row center, exactly replacing the audience member. The 3D camera is equipped with lenses and image sensors that duplicate the human field-of-view. The entire performance is photographed. There is no camera movement, no lens change, and no editing.

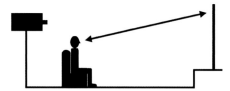

Then, that 3D movie is projected onto a screen so that the on-screen performers are exactly the same size as they were in real life. A single audience member sitting in the same first row center seat can watch the projected image and every spatial aspect of the real theatre performance will be duplicated by the 3D orthographic movie. The orthographic experience is typical for giant screen presentations and high profile thrill-rides in theme parks.

If all 3D pictures and movies were orthographic, there would be no need to discuss any additional aspects of 3D photography. The "3D police" would universally enforce the strict orthographic rules and 3D photography and display would be predictable and simple.

However, the vast majority of 3D movies and television shows are non-orthographic because filmmakers don't duplicate the shooting and viewing conditions necessary to create the orthographic condition. Filmmakers like to use different lenses, vary the image size, change the 3D settings, edit the shots together, and watch the results on any size screen. Orthographic movies are unique, fun, and extremely immersive for an audience, but non-orthographic 3D movies allow filmmakers to explore additional visual opportunities and variations.

To take advantage of these creative opportunities and visual variations, filmmakers need to understand the technical and aesthetic components of stereoscopic 3D. These components are called the 3D visual variables.

The 3D Visual Variables

Stereoscopic 3D photography offers some important new variables that are used to control 3D pictures.

1. Camera Convergence
2. Interaxial Distance
3. Stereoscopic Window

Visual Variable 1 – Camera Convergence

In traditional 2D photography, one camera with one lens is used to photograph a subject.

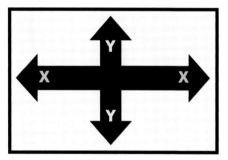

2D pictures are composed in two dimensions on the X-axis (horizontal) or the Y-axis (vertical).

In 2D pictures, the subject can be composed anywhere within the frame's two-dimensions of width and height: high, middle, and low, on the left, the center, or the right. Even when the subject appears in the distance, it's still on the flat two-dimensional surface of the screen.

In 3D photography, two cameras, each with its own lens, are used to photograph a subject.

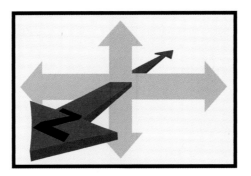

Stereoscopic 3D photography adds the **Z-axis** to the compositional choices. Now, a subject can be composed on the X-axis, the Y-axis, and the Z-axis.

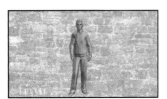  

Put on your 3D glasses and look at these pictures. In 3D, the subject can be placed almost anywhere along the Z-axis, in the foreground, midground, or background. The subject's position along the Z-axis is controlled by the 3D camera lenses' **convergence**.

In 3D, the camera lenses' convergence point or plane is always the same as the screen plane.

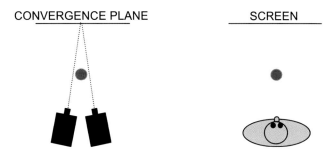

The camera lenses converge behind the subject. When viewed, that subject will appear in front of the screen plane.

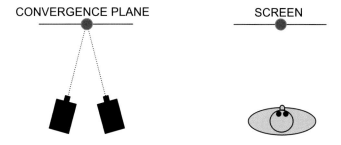

The convergence plane is placed on the subject so the subject will appear at the screen plane.

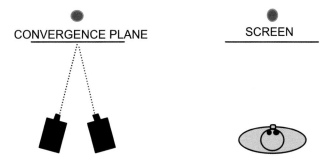

The lenses converge in front of the subject. When viewed, that subject will appear behind the screen plane.

Convergence can be used to place an entire scene anywhere in depth on the Z-axis.

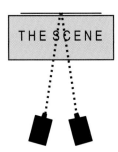 

Converging behind the scene places the scene in front of the screen plane.

Converging in the middle of the scene places it half way in front of the screen plane.

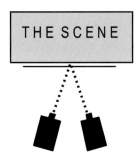 

Converging in front of the scene will place it entirely behind the screen plane.

The convergence plane does not dictate where the audience will look. Where the audience looks is controlled through composition, lens choice, lighting, staging, and action in the same way filmmakers control where the audience looks in a 2D movie.

Visual Variable 2 – Interaxial Distance

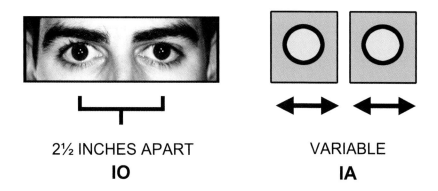

2½ INCHES APART
IO

VARIABLE
IA

Many 3D camera lenses can mimic the IO of human vision with an IA of 2.5 inches. But most 3D camera systems have an adjustable IA that can be varied depending on the needs of the shot. Most 3D photography does not use a 2.5-inch IA.

The IA distance controls:

      A. VOLUME – The three-dimensionality of objects in the shot.
      B. SCALE – The apparent size of objects in the shot.
      C. DEPTH – The total depth in the shot.

A. IA Controls Volume

Volume refers to the three-dimensionality of objects in a 3D scene. Changing the IA will affect the volume of objects. A small IA reduces volume and a large IA increases volume.

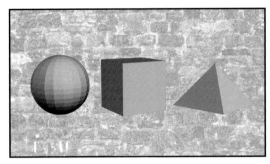

2D Shot

This conventional 2D photo of a ball, a cube, and a pyramid has no volume. The objects are round, square, and triangular but flat, like cardboard cutouts.

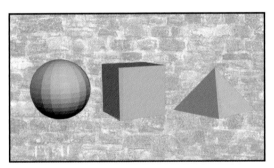

3D Shot

Put on your 3D glasses and look at this 3D photo of the same objects. The ball is not just round, it's also spherical because it has volume. The cube and pyramid now have volume along their sides.

Many factors can influence the volume of objects in a 3D movie. The lens focal length, the distance between the camera and subject, the screen size, and the audience's distance from the screen can all contribute to the perceived volume. But the most important way to control volume is by adjusting the IA.

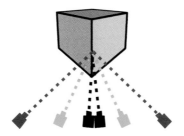

IA creates volume. In this diagram, there are three pairs of cameras looking at a cube. Each pair of cameras (a black, green, and red pair) illustrates a different IA setting. These diagrams are exaggerated to illustrate how IA and volume are linked together.

 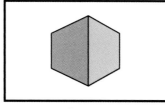 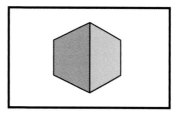

Left eye view   Right eye view

The two black cameras have a very small IA so they see nearly identical views of the cube. The cube has no volume.

 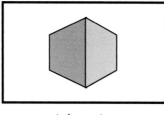 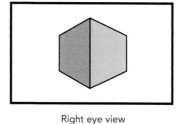

Left eye view   Right eye view

The two green cameras have a medium IA so each camera's view is different and the cube will have volume.

  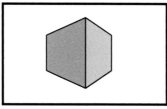 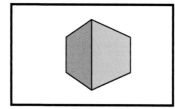

Left eye view   Right eye view

The two red cameras have a large IA and their views of the cube are extremely different. This gives the cube even more volume.

With a small IA, the two camera lenses are closer together and their views of an object are more similar.

Put on your 3D glasses. With a tiny IA the ball and head have very little three-dimensional volume. They look flat. This is usually called a shape or ***volume ratio of less than 1***. In animation this is often called less than 100 percent or ***off-model***. If there appears to be no volume at all, the volume factor is "zero."

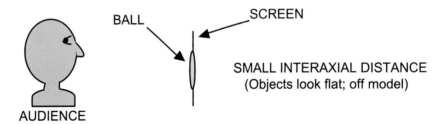

To the audience, an object photographed with a less than ideal IA looks like a flat cardboard cutout.

The IA has been increased and the camera lenses are now farther apart.

Due to the increased IA, the ball and head now appear more round and three-dimensional. The correct shape or **volume ratio is 1:1**. In animation it's called 100 percent or **on-model** volume.

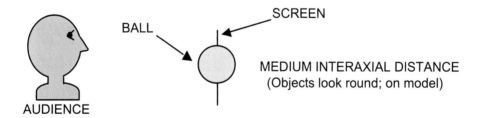

The audience sees the ball with "normal" three-dimensionality or volume.

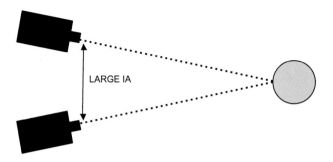

Increasing the IA further adds more volume to the objects in the shot.

The ball and head now have an exaggerated volume. They appear distorted or stretched in depth. This is called a **shape** or **volume ratio greater than 1**. In animation it's called more than 100 percent or **off-model** volume.

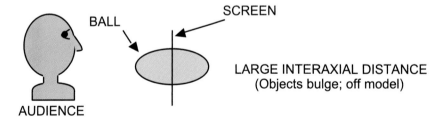

An overly large IA can increase the volume of objects too much and they appear elongated. The amount of IA needed to create good-looking volume also depends on the focal length of the lens.

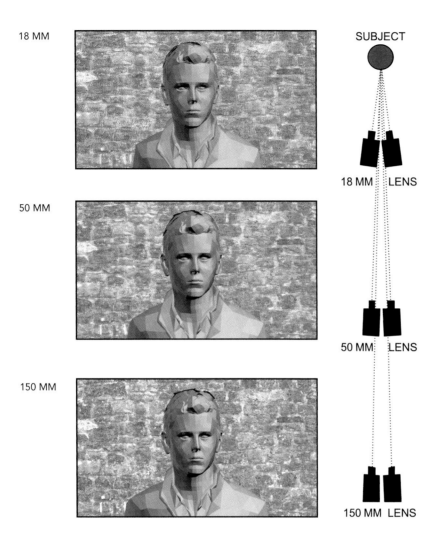

Put on your 3D glasses. All three pictures were taken with the same IA, but different focal length lenses. As the lens gets longer, the volume diminishes. The 18 mm wide-angle lens picture has good volume but the 50 mm lens has less volume and the 150 mm telephoto lens has no volume at all.

The same visual experience occurs with binoculars. Binoculars are a pair of telephoto lenses with an IA of approximately 2.5 inches. When viewed through binoculars, distant objects don't have any volume because the IA is too small. Binoculars must fit a human's IO so their IA is too small to compensate for the telephoto lenses.

To retain volume, the IA must be adjusted to the focal length of the lens.

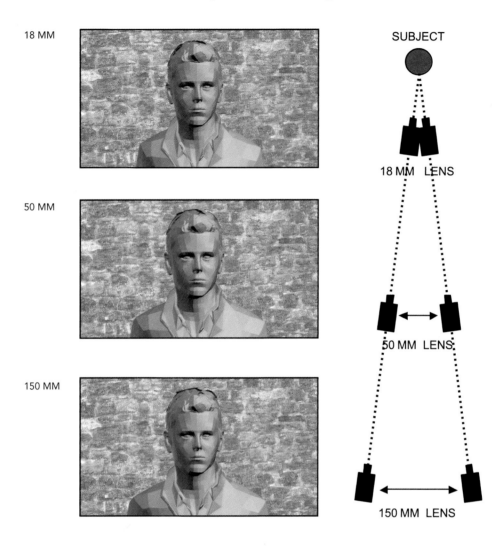

Wide-angle lenses require less IA and telephoto lenses require more IA to create volume.

In these three photos, the IA is increased as the lens focal length gets longer. Adjusting the IA will maintain good-looking volume with any focal length lens. But increasing the IA for telephoto lenses can cause problems with backgrounds.

B. IA Controls Scale

The second visual aspect that is controlled by IA is the size or scale of the entire 3D scene. A small IA may make a scene appear gigantic and a large IA may make a scene appear miniaturized.

Humans are accustomed to seeing the world with a constant IO of 2.5 inches. We can't change our anatomical IO but 3D cameras can change their mechanical IA. As the IA changes, the scale of the scene may also change. Think about smaller and larger animals that can see in 3D. A mouse has an IO of only a 0.5 inch and a grizzly bear has an IO of 12 inches. If humans are shown pictures taken with an IA smaller than 2.5 inches, like that of a mouse, the scale of the picture may feel too big. This is often called **gigantism** because the picture appears as if viewed by a tiny creature, not a human being.

Photo by David W. Kuntz

Put on your 3D glasses. This honeybee, photographed with a tiny IA, may appear gigantic. Regardless of the IA, it is already much larger than in real life so it automatically appears over-sized. A big screen makes the bee even larger, but a small IA may add to the feeling that it's gigantic. In general, gigantism is a subtle effect because audiences are culturally accustomed to oversized images on big screens in 2D and 3D. Close-ups of actors don't make them look like giants.

The opposite scale illusion occurs if the IA is too large. If humans are shown pictures taken with an IA larger than 2.5 inches, the scene may look **miniaturized** as if it's being viewed by something much larger than a human. As the IA distance increases, the scale of the picture may appear more miniature.

Photo by David W. Kuntz

Look at this photo with your 3D glasses. These full size trucks appear miniaturized because they're photographed with an overly large IA.

But gigantism and miniaturization don't always occur. In fact, 3D photography often uses an IA less than 2½ inches. A 3D scene might appear suspiciously giant or tiny because of the IA, but our brain's knowledge of the actual size of objects tends to ignore the 3D scale problems. The actual subject, the distance between the subject and camera, the lens focal length, and the size of the screen are all factors that determine how a large or small IA affects a scene's scale.

This book's small photos cannot duplicate the IA scale issues that may occur with large screens. These photos can only illustrate the general effect.

A scene's size or scale can also be affected when convergence is combined with the IA.

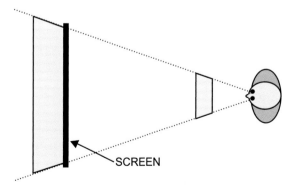

SCREEN

If a 3D scene (in blue) is positioned, using convergence, close to the audience, the scene may appear miniaturized. The same scene placed at a great distance from the audience, behind the screen, may appear oversized or gigantic.

C. IA Controls Depth

Adjusting the IA changes the total depth of a 3D scene. As the IA increases, the total depth of the scene also increases. As the IA decreases, the total depth of the scene decreases.

SMALL IA

Put on your 3D glasses and look at this shot of the three actors. This picture was taken with a very small IA so there is very little 3D depth along the Z-axis. In fact, the picture looks about the same with or without your 3D glasses.

MEDIUM IA

Now the IA has been increased and the shot has more 3D depth. The red actor appears more in the foreground and the blue actor appears more in background.

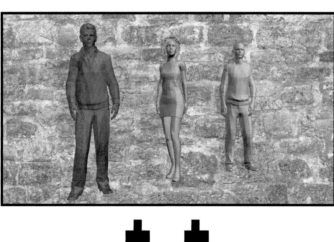

LARGE IA

Now the shot has even more 3D depth because the IA was increased again. The red actor is even more in the foreground and the blue actor is farther away in the background.

Parallax

Parallax is the difference between two camera views.

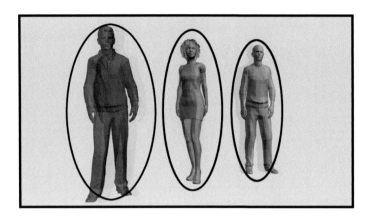

Look at this photo with and without your 3D glasses. Stereoscopic cameras photographed these actors. Because there were two cameras, there are two different views of each actor called an ***image pair***. The difference between the image pair is ***parallax***. The parallax in the red actor's image pair is easy to see. The blue actor also has an obvious ***parallax***. The green actor has an image pair, too, although it's difficult to see.

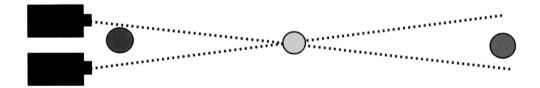

The cameras were converged on the green actor, so the image pair is superimposed over each other. The green actor has ***zero parallax***.

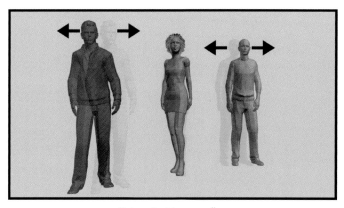

Picture A - More parallax

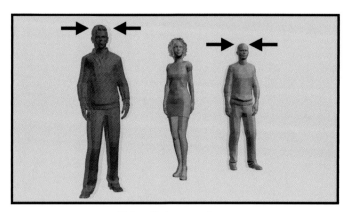

Picture B - Less parallax

In Picture A, the red and blue actors' parallax has been increased. As the parallax increases, the depth increases. In Picture A the red actor is more in the foreground and the blue actor farther in the background. In Picture B the parallax has been reduced and the 3D depth decreases. In both pictures the green actor, with zero parallax, remains in the same place at the screen plane.

Objects in front of the screen have negative parallax and objects behind the screen have positive parallax. For an explanation of why this happens, see Appendix D.

The amount of parallax in an image pair is an important factor in determining where an object will appear along the Z-axis. There are two methods of measuring the amount of parallax in an image pair.

Parallax Measurement Using Screen Percentage

This method is primarily used in live action 3D photography. Special 3D imaging software and display monitors can reveal image pairs as a visual offset.

A vertical line pattern divides the image into 50 equal parts. Each line represents 2 percent of the screen's width. A visual comparison of an image pair to the vertical lines allows the film-maker to estimate the parallax.

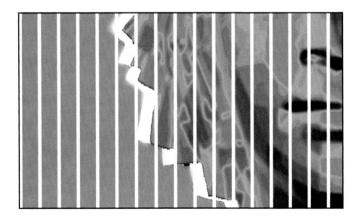

In this enlargement, the image pair offset is almost one line or about 1.5 percent parallax.

Measuring parallax using a vertical line comparison is not precise but it does quickly reveal the approximate parallax for any object in a shot. The advantage to calculating parallax in percentages is that it does not require mathematical conversion as the resolution or screen size changes.

Parallax Measurement in Pixels

The second method for measuring parallax uses screen pixels. Almost all modern 3D motion-picture projection and television transmission is digital. A digital picture is made up of pixels that offer a precise way to measure parallax. This measuring method is used in CG animation, visual effects, postproduction, and 2D to 3D conversion.

This 3D image pair has a parallax separation of 18 pixels.

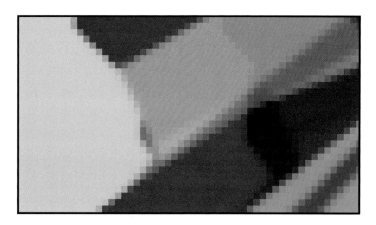

This enlargement reveals the 18 pixels of separation.

Depth Bracket

The total depth of the scene, from the nearest to the farthest object, is defined by the **Depth Bracket**. The Depth Bracket is sometimes called the **Depth Budget**.

Look at this photo with your 3D glasses. The red actor appears in the foreground, the green actor appears at the screen plane and the blue wall appears in the background.

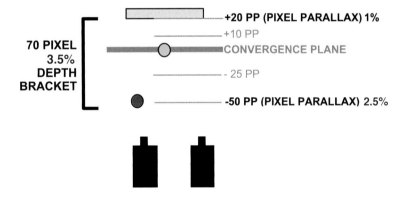

This is a diagram of the photo. The red and green dots are the actors and the blue bar is the background wall. The Depth Bracket indicates the total depth of the scene and can be calibrated in pixels or percentage of screen width. The pixel parallax of the closest object (the red actor) is –50 or about 2.5 percent of the screen width. The pixel parallax of the farthest object (the blue wall) is +20 or about 1 percent of the screen width.

The total depth is calculated by adding together the parallax of the most foreground object and the most distant background object. So, the Depth Bracket is 70 pixels (50 + 20) or about 3.5 percent of the screen's width.

The Depth Bracket's size can be adjusted by changing the IA (interaxial distance). As the IA is reduced, the Depth Bracket will shrink and the 3D depth will diminish.

The actors remain in the same physical positions but the reduced IA has decreased the amount of depth. The red actor is now at −25 pixels or about 1.25 percent and the blue wall is +15 pixels or about 0.75 percent.

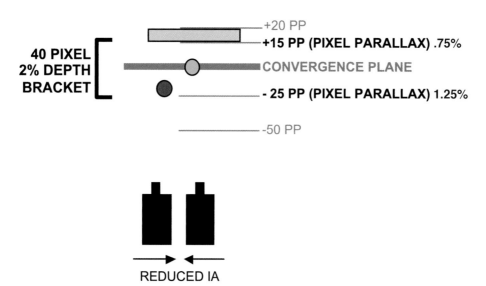

With a reduced IA, the Depth Bracket is now 40 pixels or 2 percent of the screen width.

The actors have not moved but a further reduction of the IA has almost eliminated all of the depth.

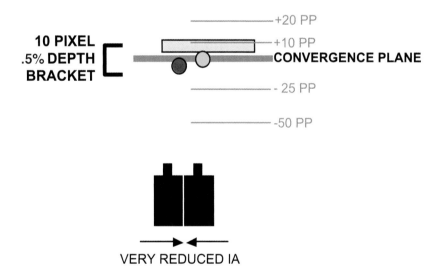

The Depth Bracket is only 10 pixels or 0.5 percent (5 pixels or 0.25 percent for the red actor and 5 pixels or 0.25 percent for the blue wall).

As the IA decreases, the volume is also reduced. Depth Bracket and volume are both affected by IA changes and cannot be separated or controlled independently during photography.

Changing the IA is not the only way to control the Depth Bracket's size. Restaging the objects and leaving the IA unchanged also alters the Depth Bracket. This will change the composition but maintain object volume.

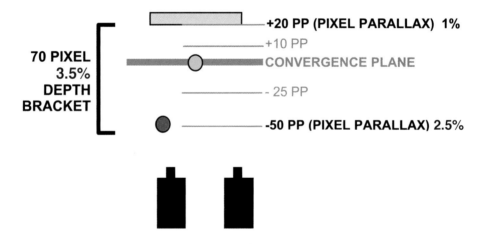

70 PIXEL 3.5% DEPTH BRACKET

+20 PP (PIXEL PARALLAX) 1%
+10 PP
CONVERGENCE PLANE
- 25 PP
-50 PP (PIXEL PARALLAX) 2.5%

The original picture and staging has a 70-pixel Depth Bracket or about 3.5 percent. Instead of reducing the IA, the actors and the wall can be physically moved closer to the convergence plane.

The scene has been restaged. The red actor and the blue wall have been moved closer to the convergence plane.

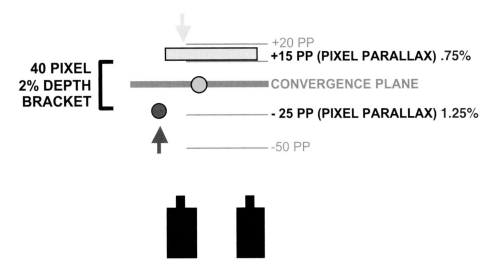

The camera's IA has not changed. The red actor and the wall have been moved (as indicated by the arrows) so the total Depth Bracket is now only 40 pixels (−25 for the red actor and +15 for the blue wall) or about 2 percent.

The scene has been restaged again. The red actor and the blue wall have been moved even closer to the convergence plane.

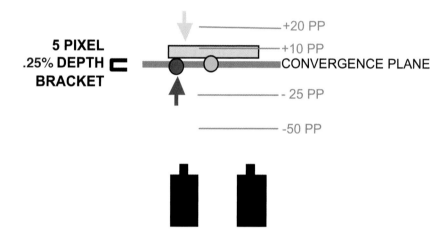

The IA has not changed. The total Depth Bracket is only 5 pixels or 0.25 percent. The shot won't have much Z-axis depth but the volume is maintained.

In the real world, your visual Depth Bracket extends from objects only inches from your face to distant stars in the night sky. Our real-life Depth Bracket is equivalent to about 2,000 pixels.

In a 3D photograph the Depth Bracket also extends from the closest to the farthest objects, but the allowable size of the Depth Bracket is much smaller than in real life due to viewing comfort issues, which are discussed in Chapter 3. The maximum viewable size of the Depth Bracket in a 3D photograph is subjective, but the largest Depth Bracket that most viewers can tolerate is approximately 120 pixels or about 6.25 percent. See Appendix B for more information on Depth Bracket size limitations.

Visual Variable 3 – Stereoscopic Window

There is a frame that surrounds every screen.

In a movie theatre it's a frame of black curtains and on a television or computer it's the plastic case that surrounds the screen. On traditional 2D movie and television screens, the frame and the screen share the same flat surface.

But in 3D, that frame becomes a window through which the audience views the world of the movie. You can create excellent 3D movies using the existing stationary frame or you can create a 3D window that floats in space.

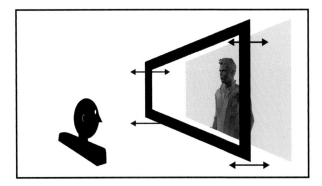

In 3D movies this new window is called the ***Dynamic Stereoscopic Window***. This window is not a black curtain but an optical mask that is part of the projected 3D image. The Stereoscopic 3D Window does not have to share the screen surface like a traditional 2D frame. It can move forwards, backwards, or tilt at a variety of angles in relation to the 3D picture. The stereoscopic window is created and controlled in postproduction.

The Stereoscopic Window (not the screen surface) becomes the threshold between two separate visual spaces.

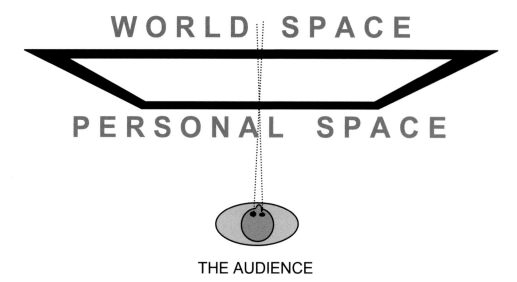

The area in front of the window becomes the **Personal Space** (or **Theatre Space** or **Audience Space**). The area behind the window is called the **World Space** (or **Screen Space**).

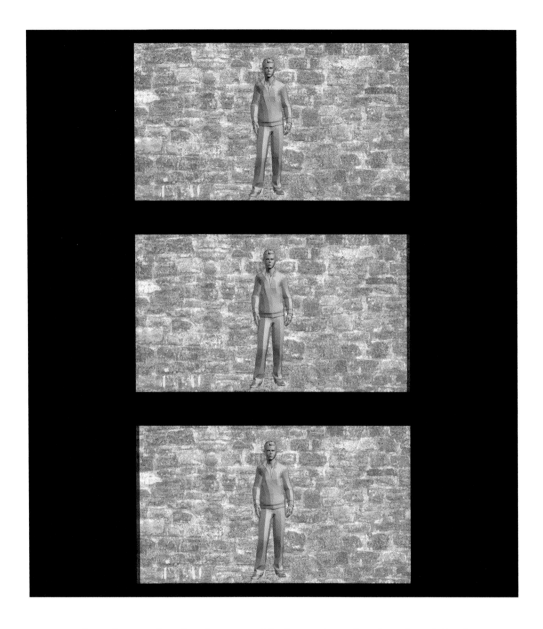

Examine these shots with and without your 3D glasses. Note that the subject's depth position never changes, but the window moves forward or back.

The Dynamic Stereoscopic Window is created by adding vertical masking to the sides of the picture during postproduction. The left-right position of the vertical masking determines if the window will appear closer or farther from the audience. The width of the vertical masking controls the distance the window moves.

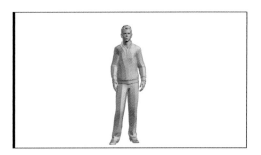 

This stereoscopic image pair has been separated to reveal how the window is constructed. In this example, vertical masking is added to the left side of the left eye and the right side of the right eye.

Put on your 3D glasses and look at the combined image pair. The additional vertical masking places the window forward from the screen (or page) surface. As the width of the additional masking increases, the window moves closer to the viewer.

 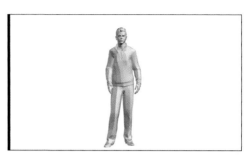

Vertical masking added to the right side of the left eye and the left side of the right eye moves the stereoscopic window farther away. View the results below with your 3D glasses.

The stereoscopic pair's added masking places the window behind the screen surface. As the width of the additional masking increases, the window will move farther from the audience.

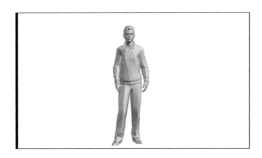 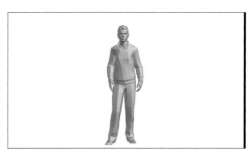

Adding masking on the left side of the left image creates an angled window. The right eye image remains unmasked. The angle of the window can be made more extreme by widening the masking.

Here's the stereoscopic window angled outward with its left side in front of the screen. The right side of the window remains at the screen surface. This angled window is often used in over-the-shoulder shots to place the window in front of the foreground actor. The window can be angled out on the right side by adding masking to the right edge of the right eye image.

The brightness and color of the window masking must match the viewing environment. Since movie screens are surrounded with black fabric, stereoscopic windows designed for movie theatres are always black. Television and computer screens present a problem because their frame (or bezel) can be a color, metallic gray, or white, which prevents the dynamic stereoscopic window from working. Any vertical edge cropping on theatre or television screens removes the stereoscopic window.

The Depth Bracket and the Stereoscopic Window

Using the Depth Bracket in combination with the Dynamic Stereoscopic Window expands the 3D creative possibilities.

The placement of the Depth Bracket and the Stereoscopic Window determines where along the Z-axis the audience experiences the 3D space. The Depth Bracket and the window can move independently or together.

Positioning the Depth Bracket in Relation to the Window

In these first examples, the Dynamic Stereoscopic Window remains stationary at the screen plane. Only the Depth Bracket position along the Z-axis changes, due to lens convergence adjustments.

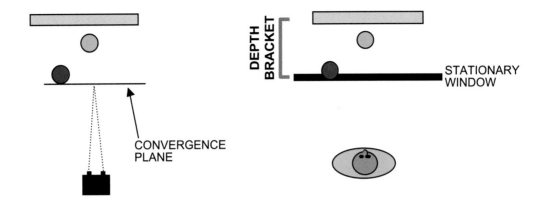

A. The convergence plane is set at the foreground red actor. When viewed, this places the entire Depth Bracket behind the window in the World Space. Picture A on page 51 illustrates this in 3D.

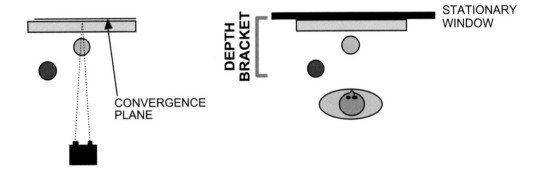

B. The convergence plane is set at the blue wall. The entire Depth Bracket will appear in front of the window in the Personal Space as show in Picture B on page 51. In these two examples, the Depth Bracket position changes due to convergence adjustments. The Stereoscopic Window remains stationary.

A. The entire scene appears behind the window.

B. The entire scene appears in front of the window.

In these two examples, the Stereoscopic Window is set outside the existing Depth Bracket.

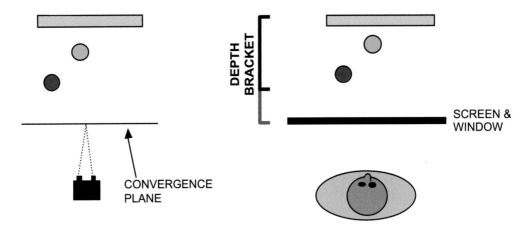

C. The convergence plane is set way in front of the red actor. When viewed, the Depth Bracket is far behind the window in the World Space. The Depth Bracket must expand (shown in violet) to include not only the scene but also the window. Picture C on page 53 illustrates this arrangement.

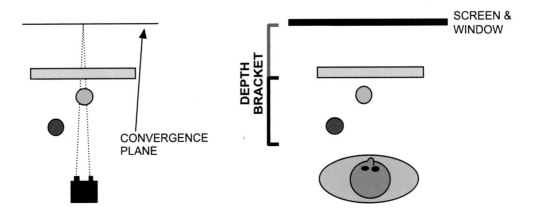

D. A similar situation occurs when the convergence is set far behind the scene. The entire Depth Bracket will appear in front of the window in the Personal Space as illustrated in Picture D on page 53. Again, the Depth Bracket expands (shown in violet) to include the Stereoscopic Window.

C. The actors and wall appear far behind the window in the World Space.

D. The actors and wall appear entirely in front of the window, well into the Personal Space.

Positioning the Stereoscopic Window in Relation to the Depth Bracket

It's also possible to move the Dynamic Stereoscopic Window and leave the Depth Bracket unchanged. This gives the filmmaker tremendous control in using the effects of the Stereoscopic Window without changing convergence or the position of the Depth Bracket.

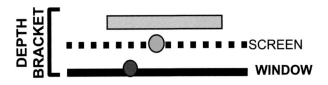

E. The entire 3D scene, indicated by the Depth Bracket, exists behind the window. See Picture E on page 55.

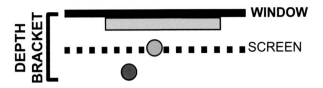

F. The Depth Bracket remains fixed. The window has moved to the rear of the Depth Bracket, placing the entire scene in front of the window. See Picture F on page 55.

E. The 3D scene exists behind the window. Only the window has been moved. The convergence and Depth Bracket size and position have not changed.

F. The window has been moved to the back of the Depth Bracket, which places the entire 3D scene in front of the window in the Personal Space.

Moving the window beyond the limits of the scene's original Depth Bracket automatically expands the Depth Bracket to include the window.

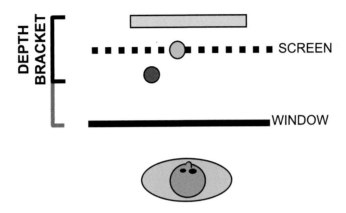

The new Depth Bracket must expand (shown in violet) to include the 3D scene and the Stereoscopic Window.

A Stereoscopic Window far in front of the 3D scene's Depth Bracket will visually expand the area in the World Space behind the window. The scene feels "deeper" because of the distance between the window and the Depth Bracket.

The side masking can be oriented in a variety of angles and proportions to reposition the entire window or parts of it. Here are two unusual Stereoscopic Windows and how they were created.

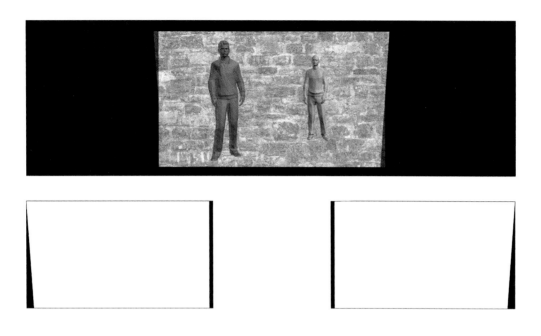

CHAPTER THREE
The Six Visual Sins

Historically, 3D movies have been associated with audience eyestrain and headaches due to technical issues and poor planning. The real problem was not eyestrain; it was brain strain. A viewer's eyes can only send images to the brain with a note attached: "Here are two pictures, figure it out." If the brain can't "figure it out" it will unnaturally realign the eyes or become confused by the two conflicting images sent from the eyes. Eventually, the brain goes into strain mode and the audience gets headaches, eyestrain, and occasionally nausea.

In 3D, there are specific technical issues that can cause audience brain strain. We'll call these problems the Six Visual Sins. They are:

1.   Divergence
2.   Coupling and Decoupling
3.   Geometry Errors
4.   Ghosting
5.   Window Violations
6.   Point-of-Attention Jumps

There are three main factors that contribute to the negative effects the Six Visual Sins can have on the audience:

1. Where is the audience looking? The Six Visual Sins can't cause problems if the audience doesn't look at them. Every shot has a subject and a lot of non-subjects. The audience spends most of its time, or all of its time, looking at the subject. The subject is the actor's face, the speeding car, the alien creature, the adorable dog etc. If the Six Visual Sins have impacted the subject, the audience sees the problem and gets brain strain.

But most of a scene is not the subject. Peripheral objects, backgrounds, unimportant characters, crowds etc. are all non-subjects that the audience acknowledges but tends to ignore in favor of the subject. Non-subjects can tolerate most of the Six Visual Sins because the audience is looking elsewhere.

2. What's the screen size? The problems caused by the Six Visual Sins can occur on any size screen, but the problems become more severe as the screen gets larger.

3. How long is the screen time? Time is critical. The longer the audience looks at the Six Visual Sins the greater the risk of brain strain. All of the Sins have degrees of strength and may cause instantaneous discomfort or take more time to have a negative effect on the audience. Brief 3D movies like those shown in theme park thrill-rides can get away with using the Six Visual Sins in ways that would be unsustainable in a feature-length movie. An audience can even tolerate the Six Visual Sins in a long movie if the Sins' appearance is brief.

Fortunately, all of the Six Visual Sins can be avoided or controlled to create a comfortable 3D viewing situation. The following discussion of the Six Visual Sins assumes the 3D is being presented on a 40-foot theatre screen.

Sin #1: Divergence

A stereoscopic 3D movie may require the audience's eyes to **diverge**. This can be a serious viewing problem and can cause brain strain.

Divergence occurs when the viewer's eyes turn outward in opposite directions to look at the subject in a scene. In real-life, our eyes don't diverge. Ever. Look at yourself in a mirror and try to simultaneously force your left eye to look at your left ear and your right eye to look at your right ear. It's impossible to do. Both eyes want to look at the same ear at the same time.

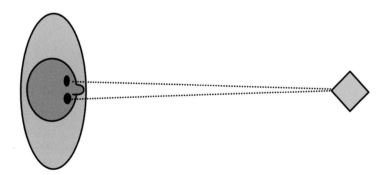

In the real world, both eyes **converge** on the same object at the same time.

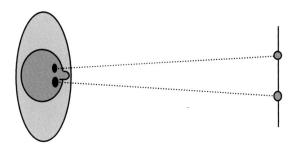

But when watching 3D, our eyes can be forced to diverge or angle outwards in opposite directions to look at an image pair. Divergence can be a problem when it involves the subject of the
shot because that's where the audience is looking.

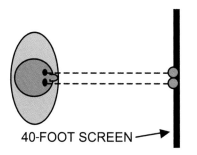

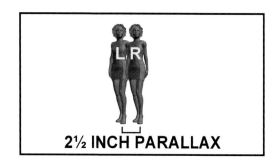

Consider how our eyes see a stereoscopic image pair for a subject that appears behind the
screen. The left eye sees the screen left image and the right eye sees the screen right image.
Human eyes have a 2.5-inch IO. If an image pair's actual measured parallax on the screen surface is 2.5 inches or less, the audience's eyes will not diverge.

On a 40-foot theater screen with 2K resolution, a 10-pixel parallax will measure 2.5 inches or
about 0.5 percent of the screen width. The 2.5-inch parallax separation forces the audience's
eyes to look in parallel but that will not cause eyestrain. In real life, we do the same thing when
we look at any object more than about 40 feet away.

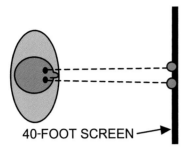

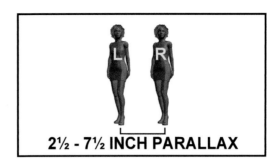

As the measured parallax widens past 2.5 inches, divergence will occur. The tolerance for subject divergence varies, but most people can watch subject divergence up to about 7.5 inches of measured screen parallax without feeling eyestrain. A 7.5-inch parallax is +30 pixels or about 1.5 percent of the screen's width.

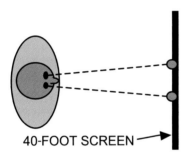

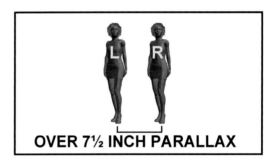

A parallax separation greater than 7.5 inches is called **hyper-divergence**. It can be used briefly for extreme subject punctuations but sustained hyper-divergence for a subject can cause eyestrain and headaches. Hyper-divergence can be used successfully for peripheral non-subjects without causing eyestrain because the audience isn't looking at them directly; it's watching the subject. Non-subject divergence can add depth that would be difficult to assign to the subject.

Watching hyper-divergence can be aesthetically distracting, and visually tiring. It's like trying to hold a heavy weight. Initially, the weight feels tolerable but as time passes your muscles fatigue, the weight feels heavier, and eventually you collapse. The same pattern occurs with hyper-divergence and it becomes visually stressful.

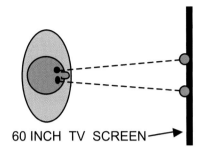

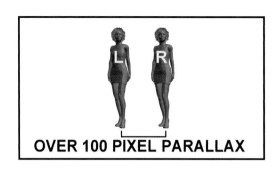

Hyper-divergence is less likely to occur on television screens. A 60-inch (measured diagonally) consumer HD 2K television has an actual measured screen width of approximately 52 inches. A parallax of +92 pixels (4.75 percent of the screen width) measures about 2.5 inches. Any background object with a +92 pixel parallax places that object at infinity, and will not cause divergence.

A pixel parallax up to +280 or 14.25 percent is theoretically tolerable but is unusable in practice because other problems occur like ghosting. In practice, a television background object's parallax of up to +92 pixels is tolerable, won't cause eyestrain, and is extremely useful directorially. Placing objects farther away than +100 (5.25 percent of the screen width) isn't necessary.

Divergence's eyestrain is actually due to a combination of screen-measured parallax and the viewer's distance from the screen. See Appendix C for a full explanation.

Hyper-divergence can cause another problem for the audience. If an object's image pair is too far apart, the audience won't be able to fuse them into a single 3D image. Even when wearing 3D glasses, the image pair appears as two identical objects rather than a single, fused stereoscopic image. The non-fused image pair visually disconnects the stereoscopic depth and the 3D illusion collapses.

Sin #2: Coupling and Decoupling

In the real world, when we look at an object, convergence and focus work together.

Convergence refers to our point-of-attention or the subject we're looking at.
Focus refers to an object being in sharp focus (not blurred).

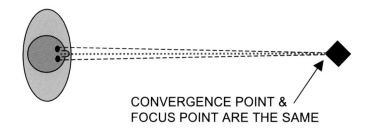

CONVERGENCE POINT &
FOCUS POINT ARE THE SAME

Our two eyes **converge** on a subject and the lenses of our eyes automatically **focus** on that same subject. Convergence and focus are **coupled**.

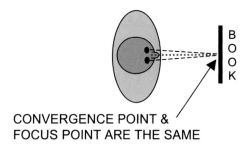

CONVERGENCE POINT &
FOCUS POINT ARE THE SAME

When you read this book, your eyes converge on a word and your eyes instantly bring that word into sharp focus. Convergence and focus are coupled and remain on the page surface.

The same coupling occurs when we watch a traditional 2D movie or television screen.

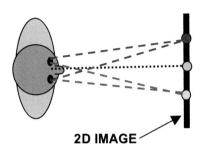 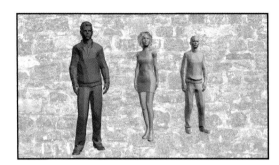

In the above 2D illustration, the blue actor may seem to be "in the distance" and the red actor may appear "in the foreground" but all of the actors are only on the page surface. Convergence and focus remain coupled together, no matter where you look within the picture.

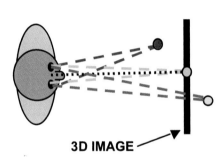 

Put on your 3D glasses. In this 3D photo only the green actor appears on the page surface. The red actor actually appears closer and the blue actor actually appears farther away.

3D pictures are presented on a two-dimensional screen, so the viewer must focus on the screen surface to make the image sharp. But the viewer may converge on an object in front of or behind the screen. Therefore, in 3D, it would seem that the viewer must **_decouple_** focus (on the screen) and convergence (on an object in front of or behind the screen). But decoupling of focus and convergence does not occur in most 3D viewing situations. Coupling and decoupling is determined by the viewer's visual depth-of-field.

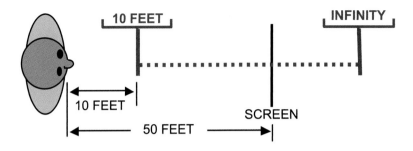

In a darkened theater, a viewer watching a 40-foot-wide movie screen from a distance of 50 feet has a depth-of-field from approximately 10 feet to infinity. Everything more than 10 feet from the viewer will be in focus.

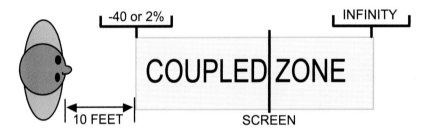

The area from 10 feet to infinity is the ***Coupled Zone***. Any object that appears within the zone will not require decoupling. The Coupled Zone extends from −40 or 2 percent in the foreground to the most distant background object at infinity.

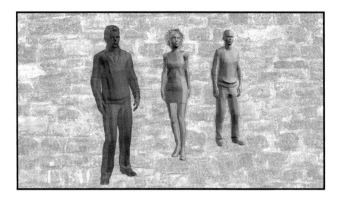

In this illustration, all three actors have been staged within the Coupled Zone.

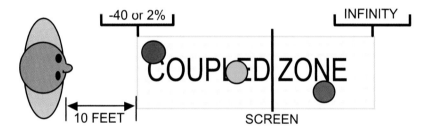

The red actor is at –40 pixels or 2 percent and the blue actor is at +10 pixels or 0.5 percent. The audience can look at any actor and their convergence and focus remains coupled.

Objects can be placed outside the Coupled Zone.

The red actor has been moved forward.

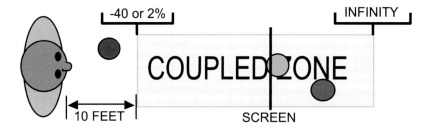

The red actor is now in the extreme foreground, beyond the limits of the Coupled Zone. Decoupling will occur when the audience looks at the red actor at –100 or 5.25 percent. Decoupling forces the audience to separate the visual mechanism for focus and convergence. Sustained decoupling, over time, can cause eyestrain.

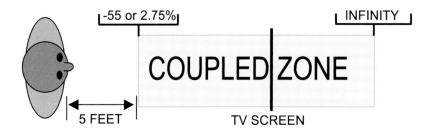

The same decoupling issue occurs with television. The viewer is 8 feet away from a 60-inch (measured diagonally) television screen. The Coupled Zone begins about 5 feet from the viewer at -55 pixels or 2.75% but no longer extends to infinity. Decoupling in television or computer screen viewing occurs more often because viewers sit close to the screen. As the viewer sits closer, the depth-of-field no longer extends to infinity.

Extreme foreground subject decoupling on any size screen is called **hyper-convergence** because the eyes are forced to look at (or converge) on a very close foreground object and simultaneously focus on the more distant screen surface. Hyper-convergence becomes fatiguing because it's difficult to decouple convergence and focus for long periods of time. The greater the decoupling distance, the faster brain strain will set in.

On a 40-foot 2K movie screen, hyper-convergence of –150 pixels or almost 8 percent creates an image pair that many viewers will struggle to fuse into a single, extreme foreground image. However, even non-fusing image pairs with extreme hyper-convergence can be used for quick visual punctuations.

The Coupled Zone can be validated by observing movie-theatre viewers who have had lens replacement eye surgery. Lens replacement patients can't change eye focus so they must rely on their visual depth-of-field to keep objects in focus. Even in a darkened theatre, lens replacement patients are able to keep objects in focus from approximately 10 feet to infinity. They can't decouple yet they can see 3D movies in depth.

Sin #3: Geometry Distortions

Geometry distortion refers to visual problems in the geometric shape of the stereoscopic pair if they are viewed or photographed incorrectly. This can lead to eyestrain or brain strain because the brain tries to realign each eye independently to compensate for the misaligned geometry.

Although the audience prefers to look at the subject, geometric distortions in non-subjects can still be a problem because they're so odd-looking that they attract the audience's attention.

Geometric Viewing Distortion: Head Position

It's important for a 3D movie audience to view the stereoscopic pair of images correctly. When watching a 3D movie, the audience must, ideally, keep their head perfectly level.

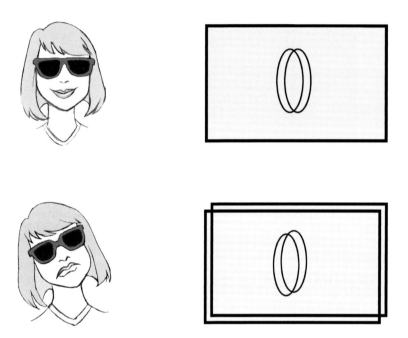

If a viewer angles or skews their head, their eyes are not level and that causes a vertical misalignment of the stereoscopic pair. The brain tries to independently realign each eye to compensate for the problem and eventually the viewer gets eyestrain.

Geometric Viewing Distortion: Seat Position

The seating position of the audience is important.

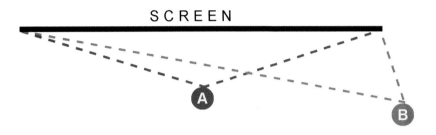

In this overhead diagram, Viewer A has the best seat because it's centered on the screen. Viewer B, sitting far to one side, sees a distorted view of the 3D stereoscopic pair.

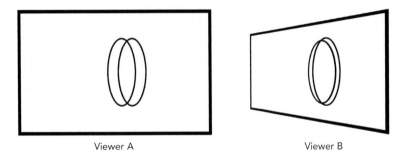

Viewer A will see the stereoscopic pair without any geometric distortion. Viewer B sees a stereoscopic pair (in an exaggerated illustration) where each image in the pair is a different size and shape. This distortion increases as the Depth Bracket expands.

Geometric Viewing Distortion: Distance From Screen

Visual fatigue caused by divergence is worse for viewers sitting closer to the screen.

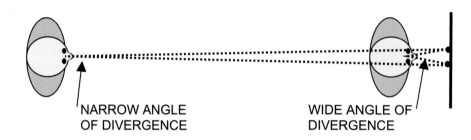

NARROW ANGLE
OF DIVERGENCE

WIDE ANGLE OF
DIVERGENCE

Sitting closer to the screen causes the viewer's eyes to diverge more when watching a stereo-scopic image pair with a measured screen parallax greater than 2.5 inches. See Appendix C for a complete explanation.

Geometric Photography and Projection Distortion

In 3D photography and display, the images in the stereoscopic pair must be perfectly aligned or **rectified**. Digital cinema has solved most of these alignment problems but they can still cause brain strain if left unchecked. Without getting too technical, here is a list of the most common problems that can provoke visual fatigue and brain strain.

1. Keystone distortion. Toe-In cameras, often used for live action 3D production, distort the stereoscopic pair.

This is an overhead view looking down on a pair of Toe-In cameras photographing a wall.

 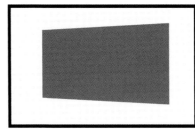

The two cameras are not parallel so each image will keystone in opposite directions (these illustrations are exaggerated to reveal the problem). This creates a stereoscopic image pair with geometric distortion. An audience will have difficulty watching image pairs with excessive opposing distortion. This distortion can be greatly reduced in digital postproduction. Using HIT cameras eliminates the problem.

2. Alignment errors. The stereoscopic pair can be misaligned vertically or rotationally.

Any misalignment on any axis is immediately difficult to watch.

3. Scale mismatch. The stereoscopic pair is not matched in size.

This occurs in live-action 3D because the cameras' prime or zoom lenses are mismatched in focal length due to a manufacturing error or incorrect calibration. A similar problem can inadvertently occur during a rack focus. Some lenses, especially zooms, may "breathe" or change focal length slightly during focus shifts, which affect the image pair's sizes. Any scale mismatch is immediately difficult to watch although the problem can be corrected in postproduction.

4. Focus inconsistencies. One image in the stereoscopic pair can be out of focus.

This problem occurs when one of the stereoscopic camera lenses is improperly focused, the lens bokeh is mismatched, or the lenses are not parallel to the image sensor.

5. Synchronization errors. 3D live action cameras must be precisely synchronized so that the stereoscopic pair is photographed simultaneously. If the cameras are even minutely out of sync the stereoscopic pair's action won't match. This turns a temporal displacement into a spatial disparity and on-screen movement looks rubbery.

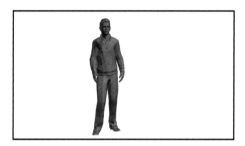 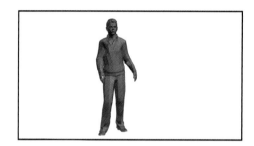

These errors are very difficult to watch because each eye receives an image from a different moment in time.

The visual geometry of the stereoscopic pairs doesn't match, which instantly confuses the perception of depth.

6. Left/right reversal. The left and right eye images of the stereoscopic pair are accidentally reversed in projection.

This problem destroys the 3D depth and is instantly impossible to watch. You can temporarily solve the problem by wearing 3D glasses upside down.

7. Reflection/polarization inconsistencies.

For a variety of technical and mechanical reasons, reflections or specular highlights may appear in one eye's image and not the other eye. This happens with objects like moving water and any shiny surface. A variety of special lens filters can help alleviate these problems. Lens flares may occur in only one lens or appear differently in each lens. Any of these inconsistencies can lead to ***retinal rivalry***, which can cause brain strain. Retinal rivalry is explained on page 86.

The retinal rivalry is easy to see when the left and right eye images are separated.

8. Lens design geometry errors. All lenses, no matter how carefully manufactured, have minute optical flaws that can distort the image's geometry or shape. These minor errors go unnoticed until two lenses are used to simultaneously photograph the same object in 3D.

9. Color or brightness mismatches. This is not a geometry problem, but the stereoscopic pair must be matched in brightness and color. Due to exposure errors or mismatched lenses, the image pair may have color or brightness inconsistencies from eye to eye.

Even minor variations in brightness can be quite uncomfortable to view. Although color inconsistencies in the stereoscopic pair are bothersome, minor mismatches may go unnoticed.

Sin #4: Ghosting

Ghosting (sometimes called **cross-talk**) appears because most 3D viewing systems cannot completely separate the left and right eye images of the stereoscopic pair. Each eye gets some "contamination" and sees a faint "ghost" of the image meant for the other eye. Ghosting is most visible in high contrast image pairs with a large parallax.

Put on your 3D glasses and look at these photos. Moon #1's stereoscopic pair shows severe ghosting because it has high contrast and a large parallax. Even with your 3D glasses on, you can still see two moons instead of one. The ghosting is less noticeable in Moon #2 because there is less parallax. Moon #3's ghosting has been eliminated by completely removing the parallax but it's lost its depth.

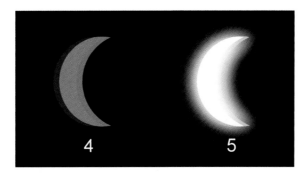

Lowering the tonal contrast between Moon #4 and the background reduces the ghosting. Moon #5 uses a glow to decrease the contrast and minimize the ghosting.

Ghosting can be reduced by art direction and lighting. Avoiding high tonal contrast in sets, locations, set decoration, and costumes can reduce the problem. A fill light can reduce the tonal contrast and add light to deep shadows to avoid the ghosting.

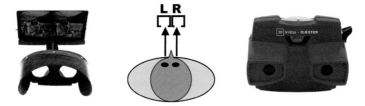

Single person 3D viewing systems, like those pictured here, eliminate ghosting because their mechanics completely isolate the image for each eye.

Sin #5: Window Violations

These violations can occur when objects appear closer than the window that is cropping the object. Window violations are more noticeable when they involve the subject of the shot. When the window is beyond the audience's field of view or involves a non-subject, most violations are difficult to notice. Window violations occur along the horizontal or vertical edges of the window.

Horizontal Violations

Horizontal window violations are visually minor because we only perceive depth information from verticals. For an explanation of this, see Appendix E. A horizontal violation occurs when an object in front of the window in the Personal Space is cut-off or cropped by the horizontal upper or lower frame of the window.

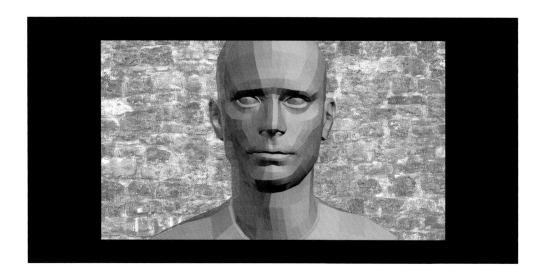

Put on your 3D glasses. The actor appears in front of the window but the actor's head and shoulders are cropped by the horizontals of the window behind the actor. The violation: how can a foreground object be cropped by a window that's behind it?

AUDIENCE

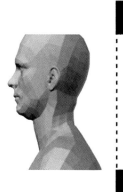

Essentially, the audience sees the screen image like this. The window is behind the actor and the actor's head and torso appear to be unnaturally sliced off. Fortunately, the audience's brain immediately compensates for this physical impossibility.

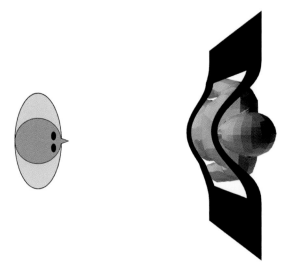

The audience assumes the window curves around the object. This is purely an optical illusion created in the audience's head. This overhead view illustrates how the audience imagines the window crops the foreground subject. There are two ways to reduce or eliminate this horizontal window violation.

SOLUTION #1: Move the entire window.

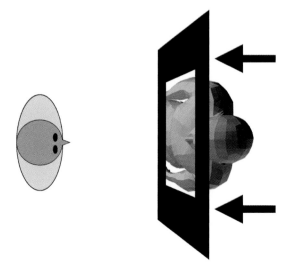

Moving the window forward in front of the object eliminates this minor window violation.

Violation   Violation Corrected

Put on your 3D glasses and look at the violation and its corrected version with the window moved in front of the actor. It's also possible to leave the window alone and move the actor behind the window, but this may create a new problem. Moving the actor back may increase the size of the Depth Bracket and create hyper-divergence in the background.

SOLUTION #2: Recompose the shot.

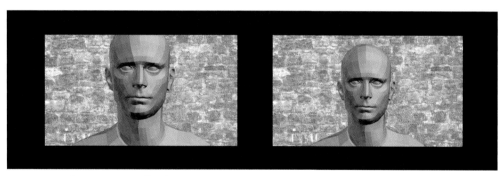

Strong Horizontal Violation   Minimal Horizontal Violation
(top & bottom)   (bottom only)

Avoid window violations that crop the subject on the frame's top and bottom. Cropping along the bottom frame line is unavoidable, but cropping on top can be minimized or eliminated.

In a close-up, the audience notices the violation because they're looking at the actor's eyes, which are near the upper horizontal frame line. The lower horizontal window violation is farther from the actor's eyes and more likely to be ignored.

Vertical Violations

Vertical window violations are more problematic because we perceive our depth information in verticals. See Appendix E for an explanation. A vertical stereoscopic window violation occurs when the vertical sides of a background window crop a foreground object.

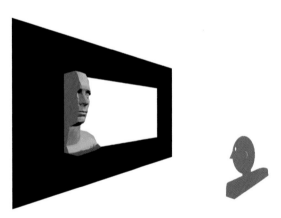

To the audience, the foreground object appears to be sliced off vertically. The basic violation is the same: how can a foreground object be cropped by a window behind it?

There are three ways this problem can be eliminated using the stereoscopic window.

SOLUTION #1: Move the entire window.

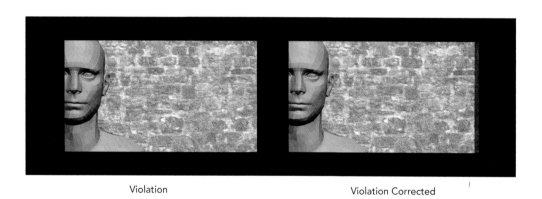

Violation   Violation Corrected

The entire window can be moved in front of the subject removing the violation. The left photo is the violation and the right photo is the correction with the window moved in front of the subject.

SOLUTION #2: Move part of the window.

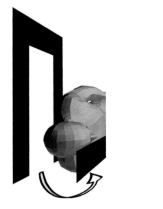 

Placing part of the window in front of the subject corrects the window violation. Most of the window remains behind the subject.

Moving one side of the window usually creates the illusion that the window is angled.

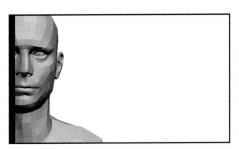 

Left eye view   Right eye view

The left side of the window was manipulated forward using the above configuration.

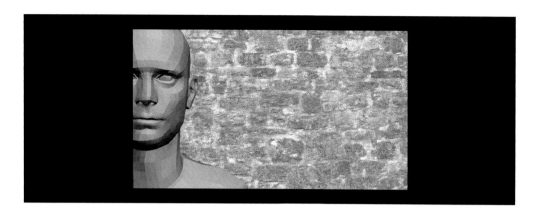

The violation has been eliminated by moving only the left vertical masking.

SOLUTION #3: Another solution is to leave the window alone and move the subject behind the window, but this may create a new problem. Like the horizontal violation solution, moving the subject back may increase the size of the Depth Bracket and create hyper-divergence in background image pairs.

Vertical Window Violations and Retinal Rivalry

Other vertical window violations can occur when the vertical frame edge blocks one eye's view of an object's image pair.

Look at this photo with and without your 3D glasses. Your right eye can see the screen left light pole but your left eye can't. You feel like you want to peek around the left frame edge to find the missing pole.

Because the pole only appears in one eye, it may seem to visually vibrate. This is called **_retinal rivalry_**. Human vision prefers to see a complete image pair; one image for each eye. When only one eye sees an image, the brain gets confused.

Retinal rivalry can be caused by inappropriate camera compositions, staging mistakes, or any mismatch in the image pair. Bright, small background objects like lights at night are particularly problematic. If the retinal rivalry involves the subject, the audience will become aware of the problem immediately. If it's only a non-subject, it may go unnoticed because the audience is looking elsewhere in the picture. There are two solutions to the retinal rivalry problem.

SOLUTION #1: Add vertical masking.

A solution is to introduce window masking over the pole's image that only one eye sees. Neither eye sees the pole and the retinal rivalry is eliminated.

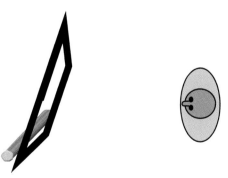

This added masking also pushes the left side of the window away from the viewer. Although the retinal rivalry problem is solved, the window placement may look odd or unmotivated.

Window manipulations can occur on the edit from shot-to-shot or during a shot. Cutting to a new shot is a perfect opportunity to invisibly change the window position. Window moves during a shot can go unnoticed if they're motivated by camera or object movement.

SOLUTION #2: Recompose the shot.

Adjusting the composition eliminates the window violation and the retinal rivalry.

Left eye view

Right eye view

The pole's image pair is now visible to both eyes.

Sin #6: Point-of-Attention Jumps

In real life there are no visual jumps. We wake up, open our eyes, and see our day like a long, continuous scene. We look at our alarm clock, our family's faces, breakfast, traffic, our work etc. We constantly decide where to look or aim our ***point-of-attention***. If we see something important, it holds our point-of-attention and becomes ***the subject***. Our point-of-attention looks for subjects all day long. Eventually, we close our eyes, fall asleep, and our continuous search for a visual subject rests.

When we watch a movie or TV screen our eyes are doing the same thing that we do in real life: they're looking for the subject. But movies and television are not as continuous or visually smooth as real life. Traditional 2D movies or TV shows have two kinds of visual jumps that interrupt our point-of-attention's search for the subject. These jumps can occur within a shot or, when we edit, from shot-to-shot.

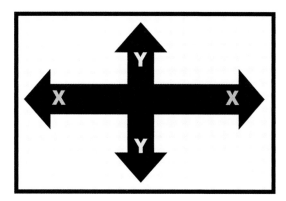

The traditional 2D screen is physically flat. There is no depth. When our point-of-attention searches a 2D picture for the subject we only move our eyes across the screen surface left to right (X-axis) or up and down (Y-axis) or a diagonal combination of the two. This is simple, easy eye movement.

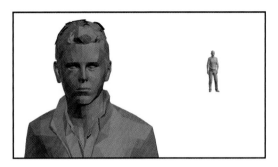

In this 2D picture, your point-of-attention jumps within the shot between the two subjects (the red actor and the blue actor).

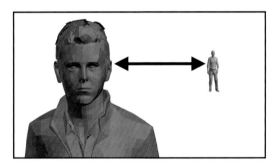

The point-of-attention jump is simply a horizontal move along the X-axis.

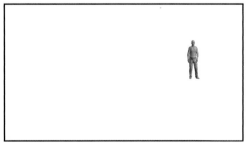

A point-of-attention jump can also occur between shots. On the edit from shot-to-shot, your point-of-attention jumps from one subject to another. Edits never happen in real life so this is a forced, artificial jump that we've learned to accept as a standard filmmaking convention.

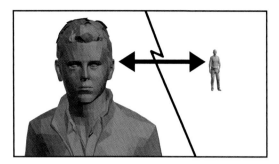

When the two shots are superimposed, the point-of-attention jump is easy to see. Even though the red actor seems close and the blue actor seems far away, both subjects are only flat images on a flat 2D screen. This is an easy and comfortable X-axis move for the audience.

3D Point-of-Attention Jumps Within the Shot

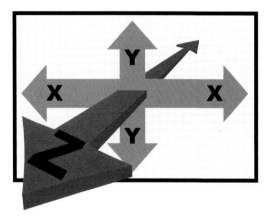

In stereoscopic 3D, the subject can be placed anywhere along the X-, Y-, and Z-axis. This can force complex point-of-attention jumps within a shot that may cause visual fatigue.

This 3D picture has two actors but there isn't a point-of-attention jump because both subjects occupy nearly the same area of the frame (on the X- and Y-axis) and the same depth (on the Z-axis). No visual jump will occur.

In this 3D shot, the two subjects' positions on the X- and Y-axis are fairly similar, but the Z-axis will require a large jump as the audience shifts its point-of-attention from the foreground subject to the background subject.

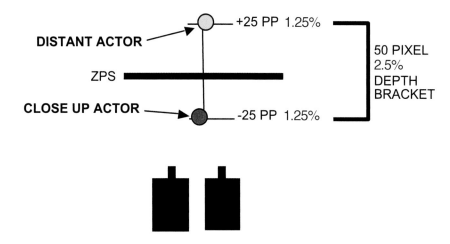

This diagram reveals the point-of-attention jump along the Z-axis. The audience will move its point-of-attention between the foreground subject at –25 pixels and the background subject at +25 pixels. The size of the Depth Bracket is a reasonable 50 pixels (2.5 percent), but the Z-axis jump will be uncomfortable as the audience shifts its point-of-attention between the two subjects.

There are four ways to avoid eyestrain caused by extreme point-of-attention Z-axis jumps within the shot:

1. Restage the scene.
2. Reduce the interaxial distance.
3. Shift the convergence.
4. Compositing techniques.

SOLUTION #1: Restage the scene.

Restaged, the scene has less Z-axis contrast.

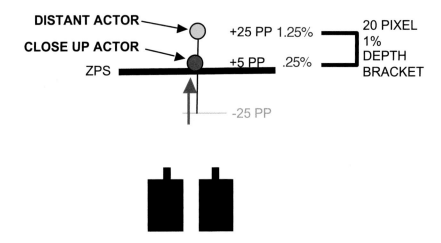

Moving the foreground actor from –25 to +5 reduces the Depth Bracket to 20 pixels or 1 percent. Now, the audience has a smaller Z-axis jump from subject to subject. This lessens the eyestrain but the shot's composition has been changed, which may compromise the shot directorially. Fortunately, there are other ways to solve the Z-axis jump problem.

SOLUTION #2: Reduce the IA. Reducing the IA alleviates the problem because it decreases the parallax in the stereoscopic pair. The actors are in their original positions but the reduced IA shrinks the Depth Bracket's size.

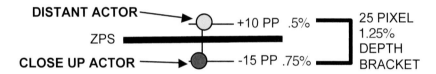

REDUCED IA

Reducing the IA shrinks the Depth Bracket to 25 pixels or 1.25 percent. The disadvantage is the objects lose 50 percent of their volume.

SOLUTION #3: The third method for reducing point-of-attention eyestrain is to shift the convergence from one subject to the other as their importance changes during the shot. The convergence shift is usually linked to the lens focus as it racks from one subject to the other.

The director must decide when the audience's point-of-attention will shift from one subject to the other and change the convergence at the right moment. This convergence technique places the more important subject on the ZPS, which is the most comfortable viewing position along the Z-axis. When done correctly, the convergence shift from subject to subject occurs simultaneously with the audience's change in its point-of-attention. This technique minimizes or eliminates the point-of-attention subject jump.

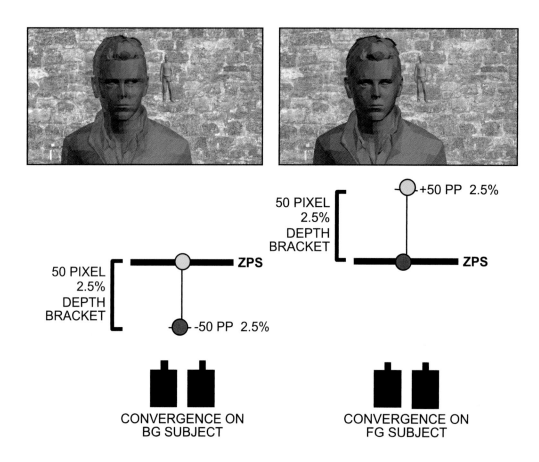

This pair of diagrams illustrates the convergence shift as the audience's point-of-attention changes from the background subject to the foreground subject. This keeps the more important subject at the ZPS. When the foreground actor is placed at the ZPS, the background subject's parallax is +50, which will cause hyper-divergence. You must be confident that the audience will ignore the background subject at +50 pixels in favor of the foreground actor at the ZPS.

The advantage to shifting the convergence during a shot is that multiple subjects can be placed at various depths without causing eyestrain since the audience never has to move their point-of-attention from the ZPS. The disadvantage is the danger of shifting convergence at inappropriate times, which will make the point-of-attention jumps worse and create eyestrain.

In general, the best technique for reducing or eliminating Z-axis subject jumps is to use all three techniques and find a combination that maintains the composition, retains good looking volume, and keeps the audience comfortable.

SOLUTION #4: The fourth technique to correct Z-axis point-of-attention jumps is to use digital compositing. Often this is done with a ***multi-rig*** technique. Multi-rigging allows each object in a shot to have independent parallax settings so the ideal Depth Bracket can be created without affecting the objects' volume or size. This avoids the side-effects of adjusting the IA, which can reduce or eliminate volume.

In CG animation, multi-rigging is a relatively simple procedure because objects are rendered separately and then composited together into one shot. This makes it possible to give each object its own IA. In live action, this same technique is used by shooting objects separately on green screen and compositing them together. This style of shooting is costly and needs to be planned well in advance.

A version of the multi-rig technique is used in the conversion of 2D movies to stereoscopic 3D. The difference is that each object in a 2D shot must be isolated by rotoscoping. Using rotoscoping, each object can be independently manipulated in depth to create the ideal 3D composition.

Before

Put on your 3D glasses. The "before" shot was photographed using a single, conventional 3D rig that photographs the entire scene at once. The point-of-attention jump from foreground to background may be too large.

After

In the "after" shot, using a multi-rig technique, the adjusted foreground actor has been recombined with the scene. The point-of-attention jump has been reduced. The multi-rig preserves the original IA and volume while reducing the parallax to keep both actors within a comfortable Depth Bracket.

The multi-rig technique cannot solve every depth problem. Spatial errors can occur if the multi-rigged Z-axis rearrangement conflicts with the reality of the shot's depth. This photo illustrates how multi-rigged 3D can look artificial. The background actor appears to be a tiny person hovering above the foreground actor's shoulder.

Manipulation of a scene using multi-rig techniques presents all kinds of typical and unique problems that occur in any postproduction compositing situation. Experience is needed to understand all of the issues involved.

Any of the four techniques (restaging, IA reduction, convergence shifts, or multi-rig) can be used in various combinations to solve point-of-attention jumps.

3D Point-of-Attention Jumps from Shot-to-Shot

Editing presents new challenges in 3D. Some filmmakers feel that the best 3D experience is to duplicate real-life vision, which has no edits at all. But editing is a necessary filmmaking tool in both 2D and 3D so it's important to understand the visual problems 3D editing can create and prevent them from occurring.

As the audience watches a series of shots in 3D, its point-of-attention will be drawn to the subject. If the subject jumps too much from shot-to-shot along the Z-axis, visual fatigue can set in.

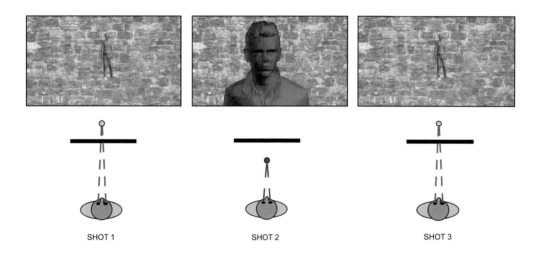

Here are three shots. The editing pattern cuts from Shot 1 (distant blue actor) to Shot 2 (close-up of a red actor), and then Shot 3 (distant blue actor). Both subjects are in the center of the screen so when these shots are edited together, the audience will not move its point-of-attention on the X- or Y-axis. But the audience will move its point-of-attention along the Z-axis to and from the blue actor in the background to the red actor in the foreground. The abrupt jump created by the intercutting of these Z-axis depth changes can create visual fatigue.

These three shots will be used to demonstrate various solutions to this problem. The visual jumps can be reduced or eliminated using one of five solutions:
    1. Accept the jump.
    2. Restage the scenes.
    3. Reduce the Depth Bracket.
    4. Subject Convergence consistency.
    5. Shot-to-shot blending.

SOLUTION #1: Accept the Z-axis depth jump. Don't fix the problem. You intend to 'jolt' the audience so the point-of-attention jump is exactly what you need.

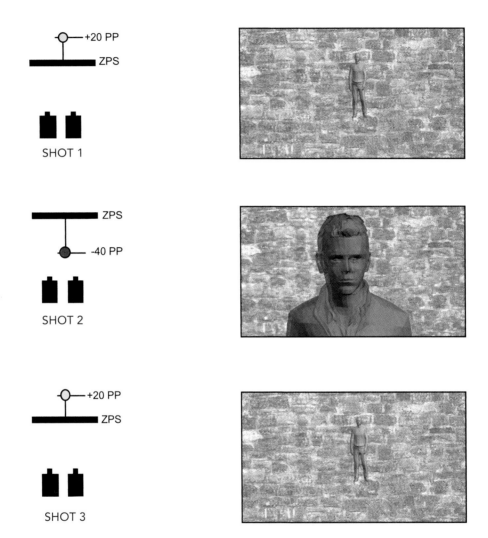

Shot 1 is a distant, wide shot. Shot 2 is a close-up designed to startle the audience. On the edit, the subject jumps 60 pixels or about 3 percent. The instantaneous Z-axis subject jump from the background to the foreground adds visual impact that the story requires.

SOLUTION #2: Restage the shots. Restaging the subjects closer together along the Z-axis reduces the subjects' parallax and the Depth Bracket's size. Of course, this also changes the shot's composition.

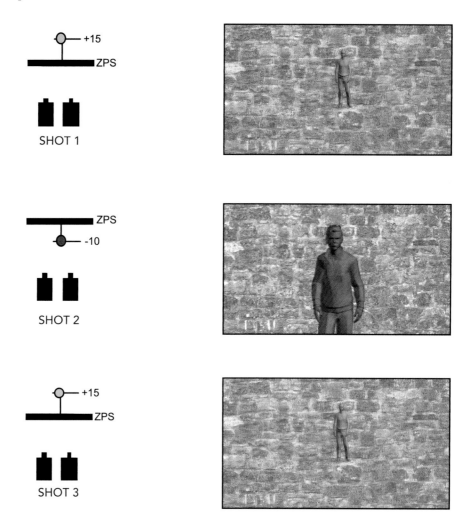

The actors are closer together along the Z-axis making the point-of-attention jumps from shot-to-shot smaller and less stressful. The subject jump is 25 pixels or about 1.25 percent. But filmmakers may find the new compositions weak and the visual storytelling compromised.

Peripheral non-subjects with larger parallaxes may remain, which can preserve a larger Depth Bracket.

SOLUTION #3: Reduce the Depth Bracket. The IA controls the size of the Depth Bracket. As the IA is reduced, the parallax for each shot decreases.

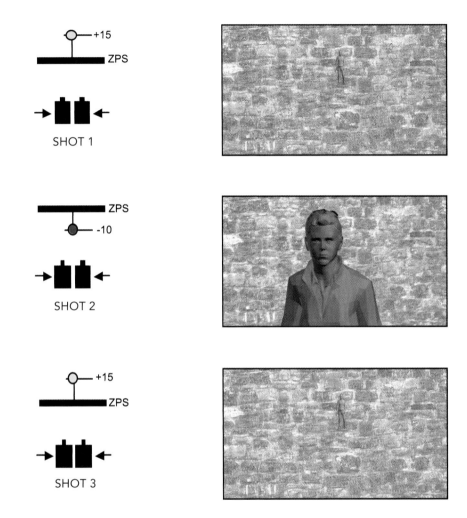

Now, the three shots have a smaller Z-axis jump of 25 pixels or 1.25 percent. But reducing the IA is always at the expense of stereoscopic volume. Too much IA reduction can eliminate volume, making objects look like flat cardboard cutouts. The IA balance between Depth Bracket size and volume is discussed on pages 128–132.

SOLUTION #4: Subject Convergence consistency. The jumps can be eliminated by keeping the audience's point-of-attention at the same Z-axis depth in every shot. This consistent depth can be anywhere along the Z-axis but is most typically set at the screen surface or ZPS.

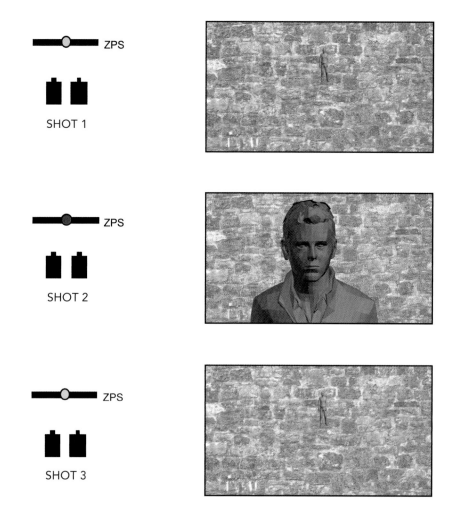

The convergence is locked to the subject, no matter where the subject is located in depth. In this example, all subjects have zero parallax and are placed at the ZPS.

The audience's point-of-attention will predictably remain with the subject. By placing the subject of every shot at the same depth, all of the subject point-of-attention jumps are eliminated. This plan is called **Subject Convergence**. Its advantages and disadvantages are discussed beginning on page 122.

SOLUTION #5: Blending. The point-of-attention jumps from shot-to-shot can be blended or softened by manipulating the convergence for each shot in postproduction using HIT. This is sometimes called **depth grading**. Blending techniques can be used in a variety of ways, which are somewhat subjective. The most effective technique will depend on the specific shots and their time length on screen.

There are three basic types of blending:
- A. Adjustment
- B. Bridge
- C. Ease-Out

Blend A: The Adjustment
Here is the problem. Edited together, these three unadjusted shots create a 45 pixel (2.25%) point-of-attention jump when seen on a 40-foot screen. This jump may be too severe and cause eyestrain.

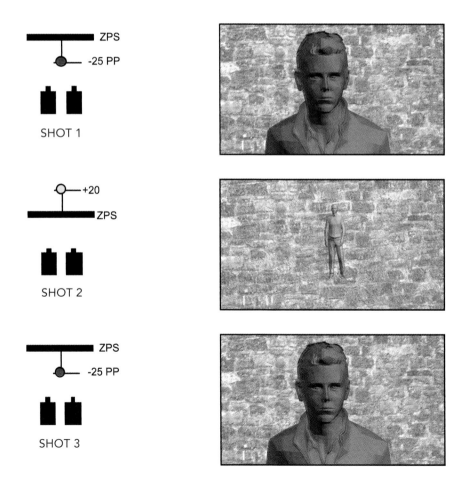

The adjustment changes the parallax of Shot 2 only. Shots 1 and 3 dominate because they're most critical to the story. Shot 2 is a less important cutaway shot.

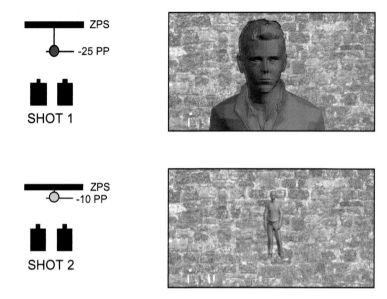

Changing the convergence of Shot 2, adjusts its parallax from +20 to −10 pixels.

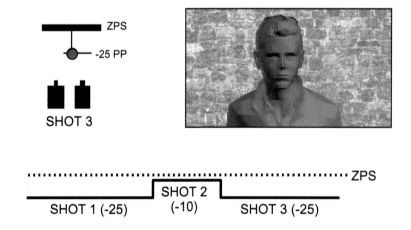

This diagram shows the blended sequence of shots. The smaller jump is more comfortable to watch and maintains a sense of depth change between shots.

Blend B: The Bridge

There is a shot-to-shot jump between Shot 1 (−25) and Shot 3 (+20).

Shot 2 will become a bridge between Shots 1 and 3.

The diagram reveals how Shot 2 will slowly change its parallax.

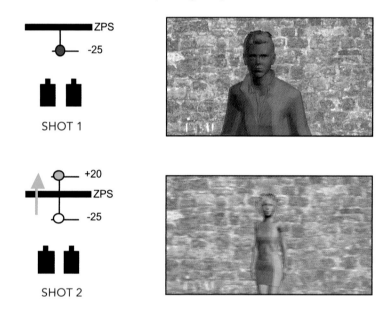

The subject in Shot 2 begins at –25 parallax (the same setting as the Shot 1 subject) and steadily changes to +20 (the setting of the Shot 3 subject). Shot 2 seamlessly bridges Shots 1 and 3 together.

Blend C: The Ease-Out

This technique is used between two shots of equal importance.

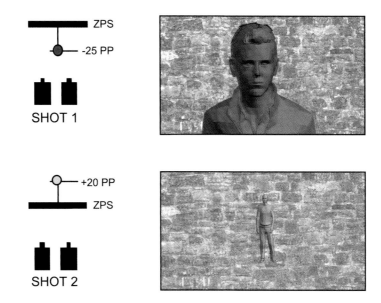

The edit between these two shots creates a potentially stressful subject point-of-attention jump of 45 pixels. To solve the problem, Shot 2 begins with a parallax similar to Shot 1 and then eases out to a parallax setting more appropriate for its own composition. Shot 1 remains unchanged.

Adjusting Shot 1 with an ease-in to Shot 2 rarely works because audiences notice the parallax manipulation. Audiences are rarely aware of ease-outs because they're acclimating to the new shot and in a few seconds the ease-out is completed.

Ideally, ease-outs are hidden by camera or subject movement. But ease-outs can be used without any visual camouflage as long as the manipulation is gradual.

Shot 1 remains unchanged. The subject of Shot 2 begins with a parallax setting of –25 pixels (matching Shot 1) and then eases-out to +20, which is the appropriate setting for Shot 2.

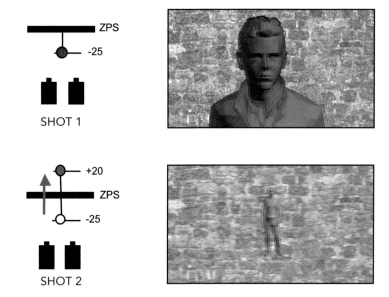

The ease-out eliminates the point-of-attention jump and preserves the preferred depth setting of each shot.

Generally, ease-outs are visually undetectable at a rate of 1 pixel per two frames. So a 45-pixel ease-out would take 90 frames or about four seconds of screen time to complete. Ultimately, the duration of an ease-out is subjective and depends on the visual specifics of the shots and their length of time on screen.

CHAPTER FOUR
3D Aesthetics

Planning the 3D

Even the simplest 3D production requires preparation. Planning a movie is like packing a suitcase.

The production team brings their ideas to the Movie-Suitcase, which is packed and closed. But wait! This is a 3D not a 2D movie. There's a new, additional stack of 3D ideas to add into the Movie-Suitcase, but there's no room. We have become so accustomed to the traditional 2D Movie-Suitcase that we resist changing our packing habits. It's easy for the 3D ideas to be left unpacked. It's time to repack, make room for the 3D ideas, and leave a few 2D habits behind.

THE FIVE STAGES OF YOUR FIRST 3D MOVIE:

1. DENIAL: My project isn't in 3D.
2. DISTURBANCE: My project looks weird and unfamiliar in 3D.
3. BARGAINING: Can I minimize the 3D?
4. RECOGNITION: Oh, 3D makes my movie better.
5. INNOVATION: You <u>must</u> see this movie in 3D.

Stereoscopic 3D can be used for two purposes. One is general and one is specific. First, there's the overall experience of seeing objects appear in depth, which is exciting and visually immersive for the audience.

By default, the introduction of the 3D into any visual structure adds intensity. Objects appearing in 3D depth do not occur in traditional 2D movies so an audience senses these changes as visual intensity. So, 3D can be used simply to increase visual intensity in a sequence or an entire movie. But 3D can serve a second, more precise purpose.

A 3D plan can be created that parallels and supports the storytelling. Specific story situations, relationships, and conflicts can be enhanced visually by controlling the 3D. The filmmakers can orchestrate a unique relationship between the story structure and the 3D visual structure. This kind of planning and control adds richness to the storytelling and creates a unique and interesting 3D visual style. Is your 3D plan living up to the expectations of your paying audience?

This chapter deals with directing and designing the 3D movie.

Viewing 3D Images

In the early stages of design, the first question is often: where are the pictures going to be seen? In traditional 2D picture-making, a webisode will be approached differently than an IMAX movie. Likewise, a 3D movie cannot be designed to look great on all screen sizes. The most effective 3D movies are designed for a specific sized screen and a preferred audience viewing position, but there is a lot of latitude in what works for the audience.

Good 3D planning requires experience. Designing 3D pictures using a small screen and presenting them on a large screen is dangerous. If parallax settings have been calculated for a small screen, these settings will be magnified on a large screen and may go beyond comfortable viewing limits. Conversely, designing 3D for a large screen and then viewing it on a small screen reduces the parallax, which reduces the 3D depth. This will be comfortable to watch but won't have much 3D.

The size of the screen and the audience's distance from the screen has a direct effect on how the 3D looks.

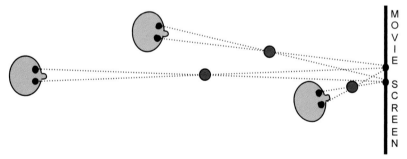

On a 40-foot screen with 2K resolution, it takes only –10 pixels (0.5 percent) of parallax to place an object halfway between any viewer and the screen surface. Human eyes are 2.5 inches apart and 10 pixels of parallax equals 2.5 inches of measured screen width. Negative parallax requires the viewer's eyes to cross their line of sight when viewing an image pair.

As the diagram shows, every audience member's crossover point (where the object will appear) is halfway between that viewer and the screen. No matter where you sit, the same 3D object will always appear halfway between you and the screen. Sitting closer to the screen makes the object more aggressive, immediate, and immersive. Sitting farther away stretches the depth out into a deeper space but keeps the 3D objects at a distance and is not as immersive.

Sitting close to the 3D screen compresses the depth but creates a more immersive visual experience because the picture fills the viewer's field of view and the edges of the screen may go unnoticed. IMAX 3D can be extremely immersive because the giant screen easily fills the audience's field of view and the screen edges are often beyond its peripheral vision.

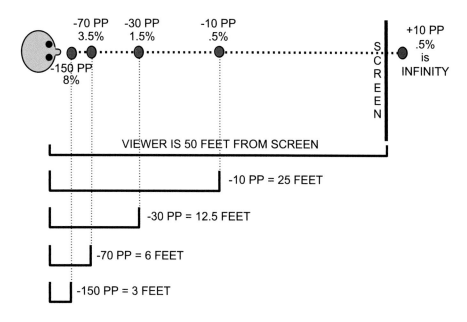

40-FOOT MOTION PICTURE SCREEN
2K RESOLUTION

There is a non-linear relationship between parallax and apparent distance from the viewer. This illustration uses a viewer sitting 50 feet from the screen. A parallax of −10 (0.5 percent) places an object at half the viewer's distance from the screen, or 25 feet away. A parallax of −30 (1.5 percent) moves the object twice as close or 12½ feet from the viewer. A parallax of −70 (3.5 percent) moves the object to only 6 feet away. At a parallax of −150 (8 percent), the object appears 3 feet from the viewer.

It takes approximately −200 pixels of parallax to place an object easily within arm's reach of the audience. A parallax of only +10 pixels (0.5 percent) places an object at infinity behind the screen.

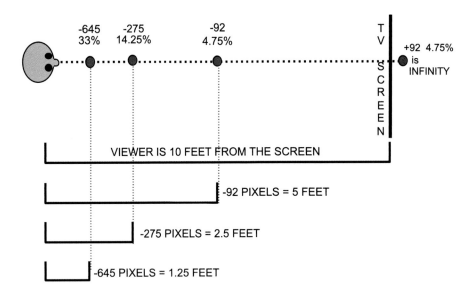

60-INCH TV SCREEN
2K RESOLUTION

On a 60-inch (measured diagonally) 2K HD television screen the numbers are different although the principle is the same.

This illustration uses a viewer sitting 10 feet from the TV screen. It takes –92 parallax (4.75 percent) to place an object halfway between the viewer and the television screen, or 5 feet from the viewer in this example. A –275 pixel parallax (14.25 percent) puts the object only 2.5 feet from the viewer. A parallax of –645 pixels (33 percent) places an object easily within arm's reach but will be unwatchable for various technical reasons. An object can be placed at infinity with a parallax of +92 pixels (4.75 percent).

Object volume will look different depending on the viewer's distance from the screen.

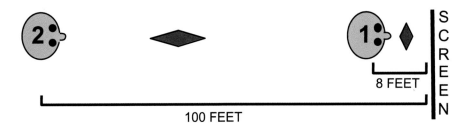

Viewer 1, sitting close to the screen, will see less volume in objects. Viewer 2, sitting farther from the screen, will see the same objects with more volume.

Optimum viewing distance for a 3D movie theatre screen is approximately the width of the screen. If the screen is 40 feet wide, the best viewing location is about 40 feet away. Television viewing distance is approximately 2.5 times the screen width. For a 60-inch HD 2K television screen (actual measured width is 52 inches) the best viewing distance is about 10 feet.

When you're new to 3D, it's important to preview your work in 3D on a screen size that is identical to its intended final format. Using a small television monitor will misrepresent 3D that's designed for a large theatre screen.

3D should not be evaluated by stopping on a "freeze frame" and analyzing a scene's depth. The depth details of a 3D movie should be judged when the footage is running at normal speed on an appropriately sized screen.

When editing, 3D footage should be viewed more often than you would in 2D. This allows the film-makers to check for 3D effectiveness and viewing comfort. As you become more accustomed to 3D and understand its unique visual qualities, it gets easier to see problems on any size monitor.

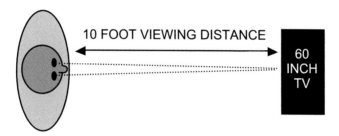

A viewing distance of approximately 10 feet from a 60-inch (measured diagonally) HD 2K monitor will simulate the 3D volume of the same images on a 40-foot movie screen. But a small monitor cannot be used to properly evaluate visual emersion, parallax, Depth Bracket, or convergence intended for a larger screen.

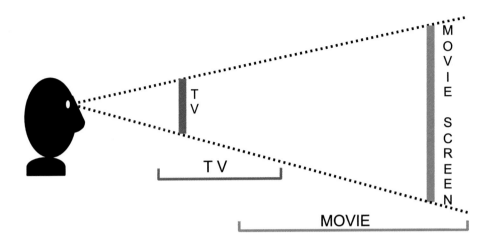

Viewers usually sit closer to a television screen and farther from a movie screen. The Depth Bracket for TV tends to have less in front and more behind the screen. This helps to offset miniaturization, which is a constant problem in 3D television presentations. A theatrical movie should place the Depth Bracket more in front and less behind the screen. These Depth Bracket placements are only a general suggestion and not a rule.

Aspect Ratio in 3D

There are two traditional aspect ratios in 3D. Although 2.40 is often called "widescreen" and sounds more appropriate for 3D, those proportions eliminate the important upper and lower areas of the frame, which are very useful in 3D.

2.40 ASPECT RATIO

1.85 ASPECT RATIO

Many directors and cinematographers feel that a 1.85 aspect ratio is more useful for 3D because it offers additional compositional height to include more 3D depth. The added height can also allow the scene to move into the Personal Space more easily.

2D aspect ratios only account for the horizontal and vertical frame relationship. 3D aspect ratio involves the horizontal, vertical, and depth proportions, or the X-, Y-, and Z-axis relationship.

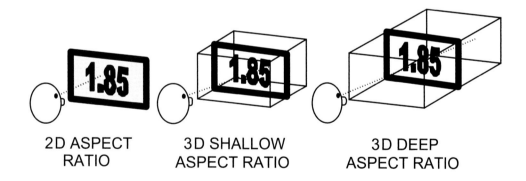

2D ASPECT
RATIO

3D SHALLOW
ASPECT RATIO

3D DEEP
ASPECT RATIO

The 2D aspect ratio of 1.85 is a simple rectangle with only a two-dimensional height and width limitation. But in 3D, the 1.85 aspect ratio becomes a two-dimensional window suspended inside a three-dimensional box. The box is actually called a **frustrum** and is shaped like a four-sided pyramid, but to keep things simple we'll leave it as a box.

Filmmakers must learn how to use the "depth of the box," which is also the Depth Bracket. The Depth Bracket can be shallow or deep depending on the story, the design of the film, and the imagination of the production team. A variety of visual choices can affect the size of the Depth Bracket or the "depth of the box."

Placing the Subject in Depth

Compositionally, there is an aesthetic question about where to place the subject in depth. Should a "close-up" bring the subject closer to the audience? Should a wide shot of distant mountains place them far away or not? Where, within the depth of the three-dimensional box, do you place the subject of the shot? And once you decide where you want the subject, how, technically, do you get it there?

Adjusting the IA will, in a minor way, affect the subject's depth position. But convergence is the best way to place a subject anywhere in the "depth of the box."

In the design of a 3D movie, there are three convergence styles for controlling the subject's placement.

1. Shot Convergence
2. Subject Convergence
3. Adaptive Convergence

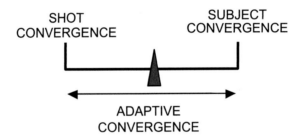

Shot Convergence sets the convergence plane based on the entire 3D composition. Subject Convergence always sets the convergence on the subject. Adaptive Convergence uses a combination of the two and places the convergence plane where it's best suited for the story and 3D design.

1. Shot Convergence

Using Shot Convergence, a single setting is found that places the entire composition at the most appropriate depth position along the Z-axis.

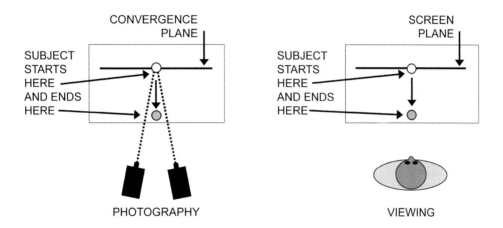

In photography, the convergence is set three-quarters of the way into the depth of the scene. When viewed, most of the scene will appear in front of the screen plane. As the subject walks forward towards the camera, the convergence is not changed. When viewed on a screen, the subject will move closer to the audience.

Put on your 3D glasses. These two photos illustrate the Shot Convergence diagrams. The subject (actor) starts farther away, walks forward, and gets closer to you. The Z-axis movement in depth that occurred in front of the camera is duplicated when viewed.

PROS: The subject's movements in 3D depth will appear similar to what happens in real life. As the subject moves along the Z-axis closer or farther from the camera, the subject will move closer or farther from the viewing audience, enhancing the 3D experience.

CONS: Shot Convergence can cause Z-axis subject point-of-attention jumps from shot-to-shot that may become visually stressful. These jumps may require shot-to-shot blending.

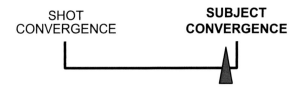

2. Subject Convergence

In this second technique, convergence is locked to the subject. The convergence is constantly adjusted to keep the subject on the convergence plane, no matter where the subject moves along the Z-axis. This technique is identical to adjusting or racking focus as the subject moves within the depth of a shot. Subject Convergence is dependent on directorially defining the subject and constantly converging on that subject. If the subject changes during a shot, the convergence is adjusted to the new subject.

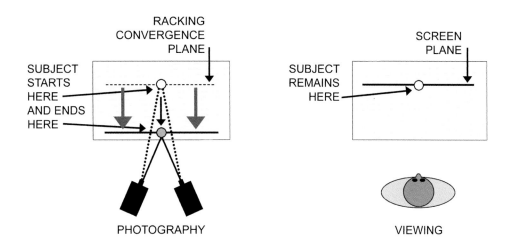

In photography, the convergence begins on the subject, who is three-quarters into the depth of the scene. As the subject moves forward along the Z-axis, the convergence is adjusted or racked to follow the subject (indicated by the red arrows). When viewed, the subject remains on the screen surface, no matter where the subject moves in depth along the Z-axis.

Actor at Convergence Plane   Actor remains at Convergence Plane

Put on your 3D glasses. In these illustrations, as the subject walks forward along the Z-axis towards the camera, the convergence is adjusted to keep the subject on the convergence plane. No matter where the subject moves in depth, it remains at the screen plane or ZPS when viewed.

PROS: The advantage to this technique is that the subject of every shot remains at the screen plane, which eliminates most of the Six Visual Sins. In particular, there won't be any shot-to-shot point-of-attention subject jumps so shots can be edited together in any order and provide a comfortable viewing situation for the audience.

CONS: This technique eliminates variety in the subject's depth along the Z-axis. For the audience, the subject will never appear closer or farther away. A close-up face will get bigger, but not closer, as it does in a 2D movie. A distant subject may appear small on the screen but it won't actually be any farther away than the screen surface. When using Subject Convergence, it's essential to maximize the depth in non-subject and peripheral objects to create and maintain a compelling 3D space.

Directorially, the placement of the subject can use Shot Convergence or Subject Convergence. An actor can be placed in the distance using Shot Convergence or placed on the ZPS using Subject Convergence. Put on your 3D glasses and look at the following picture pairs. Each pair illustrates how a subject looks using Shot Convergence and Subject Convergence.

Shot Convergence   Subject Convergence

Shot Convergence   Subject Convergence

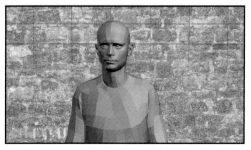

Shot Convergence   Subject Convergence

3. Adaptive Convergence

The third technique is a combination of both types of convergence.

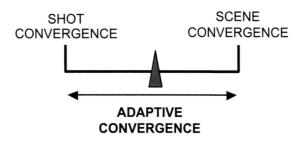

Shot Convergence may be the right choice for a particular shot, scene, or sequence. During the story, it may be appropriate to switch plans and use Subject Convergence. This choice relies on understanding the story and picking the most appropriate type of convergence.

The audience watches the subject of your shot. They will certainly be aware of the backgrounds and peripheral objects, but their primary attention will be on the subject. Do you want the subject to be an active part of the depth? Do you want the subject to be surrounded by the depth? Or do you want a combination of Shot and Subject Convergence?

Drifting between the two in an organic way may be the best solution. This basic decision will affect the staging of actors, the camera angles, the production design, and the technical approach to the 3D.

PROS: You get the best of both worlds. You can avoid the Six Visual Sins using Subject Convergence, but when you need it there can be interesting visual depth provided by the subject of the shot using Shot Convergence.

CONS: Adaptive Convergence requires more skill and planning.

Convergence and the Stereoscopic Window

The Stereoscopic Window can be used in conjunction with either Shot or Subject Convergence to enhance the depth.

Shot A   Shot B

These two Subject Convergence shots look similar but they're not. In Shot A, the subject and the window are both at the ZPS. In Shot B, the subject remains at the ZPS but the window has been pushed back behind the subject. This creates the illusion that the subject has moved forward, but the subject's Z-axis position actually remains unchanged.

There are times in a story when deliberately reversing or manipulating the 3D space can be useful. By placing the Depth Bracket and window at inappropriate distances (too near or too far), the space can become visually disorienting or add intensity to a shot.

Put on your 3D glasses. The distant actors have been brought forward into the Personal Space and the close-up actor has been pushed into the deep background. Either of these spatial manipulations may be perfectly appropriate for certain kinds of storytelling.

Conforming the 3D to the real-life experience of depth may seem obvious or even boring. But 3D is an important visual cue that allows an audience to understand the geography of the space, the physical relationship of the objects in the space, and the position of the camera. Duplicating the way we perceive space in the real world is important to keeping the audience acclimated and involved in a 3D movie.

The Big Choice

As you plan your 3D, you'll have three variables to consider:

1. DEPTH BRACKET: You'll want a Depth Bracket that's comfortable to watch.
2. LENS CHOICE: You'll want to use any focal-length lens.
3. VOLUME: You'll want objects to have a consistent, good-looking volume.

But these three variables are interconnected. There is a direct relationship between the Depth Bracket, the lens choice, and volume.

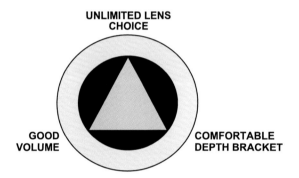

MAINTAIN A COMFORTABLE DEPTH BRACKET: The Depth Bracket determines the amount of 3D space in your shots. Finding a comfortable Depth Bracket for the audience's viewing is important. If the Depth Bracket gets too large it creates hyper-divergence and hyper-convergence, which are uncomfortable to watch.

USE ANY FOCAL LENGTH LENS: Every camera comes with an amazing range of lenses and part of our visual language is the ability to use them all. You want to pick any lens without limitation.

MAINTAIN GOOD-LOOKING VOLUME: Object volume should look good from shot to shot. Although there is leeway in what the audience will accept as good-looking object volume, it should seem consistent and not draw attention to volume errors or mismatches.

THE VARIABLE CHOICE: The interesting relationship between these three variables is that you can control any two but not all three, so you must find a balance between them.

This is easier to understand with a chart. Here are the variables in three columns:

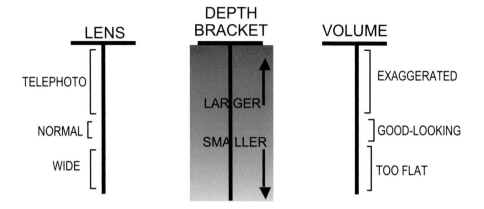

The lens choices are: Telephoto - Normal - Wide Angle. The Depth Bracket size choices are: Larger - Smaller. The Depth Bracket column is also marked in red (uncomfortable to watch) and green (comfortable to watch). The volume choices are: Exaggerated - Good-Looking - Too Flat.

You have control over any two variables, so pick two and draw a straight line through all three columns.

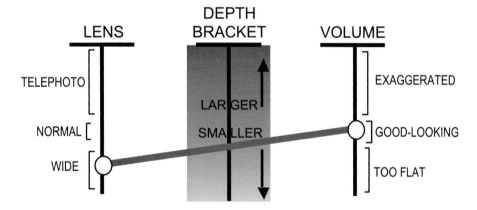

Choose a wide-angle lens and good-looking volume (the yellow dots). Draw a straight line and you'll see what size Depth Bracket you'll get. The Depth Bracket remains in the green area, not too large and comfortable to watch. Good choice.

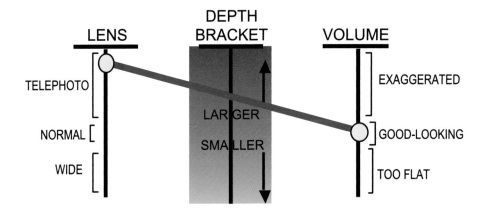

Pick two different variables. If you choose a long telephoto lens and good-looking volume, the line reveals a problem. The Depth Bracket goes into the red zone and your 3D pictures will be uncomfortable to watch. You can't use long lenses, have a comfortable Depth Bracket, and good-looking volume at the same time. Bad choice.

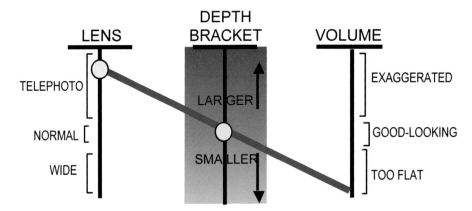

To keep the telephoto lens, you can choose to reduce the size of the Depth Bracket, which puts the straight line back in the green area. But now there won't be any volume. Remember, you can only control two of the three variables.

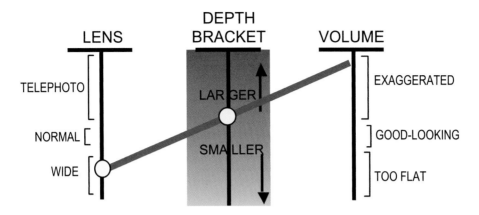

Pick a wide lens and a larger Depth Bracket. The straight line indicates that the volume will be exaggerated.

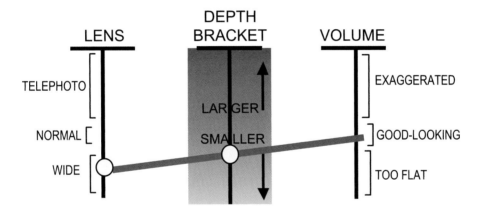

Picking a wider lens and a smaller Depth Bracket helps to maintain good-looking volume.

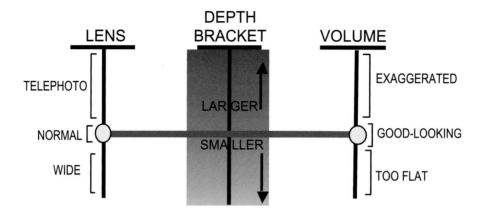

If you use normal lenses and want good-looking volume, you could begin to move into the red area of the Depth Bracket. Where that exact threshold begins is subjective and depends on the consensus of your production team.

Specific lens focal lengths have been left off this chart on purpose because focal lengths vary depending on the size of the camera's imaging chip. Good-looking volume is somewhat subjective and has some visual leeway. If 100 percent volume is "normal," an audience usually accepts any volume from 70 percent to 130 percent as being good-looking.

The 2D Depth Cues in 3D

The traditional 2D depth cues, developed through centuries of drawing, painting, and modern photography are visual tricks to create the illusion of depth on a flat, two-dimensional canvas. Those same depth cues (with the addition of movement) are used to create the illusion of depth in 2D photography.

In 3D, the illusion of depth is more real. A 3D stereoscopic system can photograph the actual depth of a space and reproduce it for an audience.

It is absolutely critical to understand that 3D can only amplify the actual depth that is in front of the camera. Employing the depth cues insures that a shot has actual depth that can be recognized by the 3D photography. These depth cues must be employed in scene staging, composition, camera placement, lens choice, lighting, and production design.

Here is a breakdown of the traditional depth cues as they apply to 3D picture-making. These depth cues are essential to creating space that exploits 3D.

1. Object Placement in Depth

Z-axis staging of actors and objects is critical to creating the 3D experience.

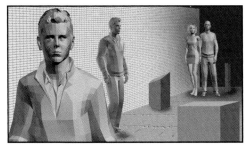

X- and Y- Axis Staging

X-, Y-, and Z- Axis Staging

Staging only on the X- and Y-axis does not create depth in front of the camera so there's not going to be much, if any, depth in the 3D photography. When the staging uses the Z-axis, the 3D photography can reveal or enhance the depth. Although it seems obvious, this is often the most ignored depth cue in 3D production. If the scene doesn't use the Z-axis, the 3D photography cannot add depth that was never there in the first place. Placing actors and objects in depth also activates many of the other depth cues. Appendix F lists some traditional 2D movies that are excellent examples of staging in depth.

3D photography can reveal depth that remains hidden in traditional 2D photography.

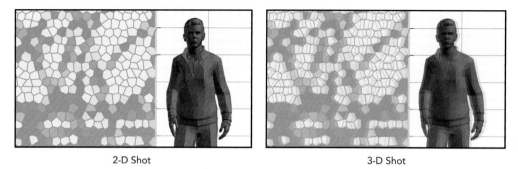

2-D Shot   3-D Shot

Here's the same shot in 2D and 3D. In 2D, the wall appears to be a flat panel. The 3D reveals there are two walls in depth.

2-D Shot   3-D Shot

The same thing happens with patterns and textures. In 2D, a mass of trees is only a flat texture. But in 3D the trees separate into different depths.

2. Visual Density

This a unique, critically important depth cue, which affects all of the other cues.

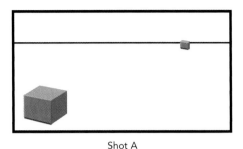   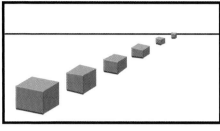

Shot A   Shot B

Visual density refers to the presence of objects that reveal the other 3D depth cues.
Shot A, with very few objects, may only convey a minimal amount of 3D depth. Shot B, with more visual density, activates and reveals more 3D depth.

Visual density also leads the audience's attention deeper into the scene and reduces the visual stress from subject jumps along the Z-axis. In Shot A your eye abruptly jumps from the foreground to the background. In Shot B, the row of boxes guides your eyes in a smooth transition, like a "visual handrail," from the foreground to the background.

Look at these shots with your 3D glasses. The empty parking lot lacks visual density. When the shot is dense with cars, the 3D depth becomes much more apparent.

3. Camera Movement

There are three camera moves that enhance depth. In live-action production these moves are tracking left and right, the dolly forward and back, and craning up and down. CG software calls these camera moves "translations." Any of these camera moves add depth because they create **relative movement**. Relative movement is the perceived speed changes between the foreground, midground, and background.

Track left and right

The camera moving left or right creates relative movement.

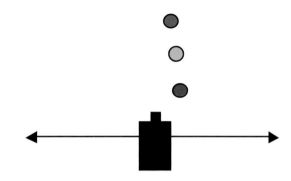

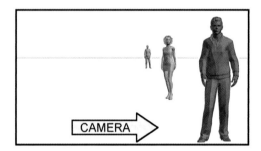
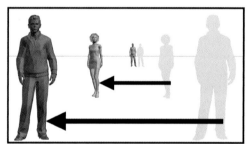

In this example, the camera dollies to the right, in front of foreground, midground, and background objects. As the camera dollies, the foreground object will move the fastest, the midground will move slower, and the background object will move slowest. The audience sees this relative difference in object speeds and perceives depth.

Dolly in and out

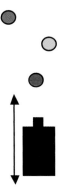

Relative movement is also created when the camera dollies towards or away from the subject.

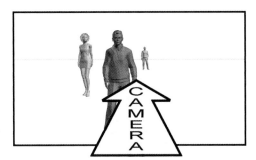 

As the camera dollies in, the foreground moves the fastest, the midground moves slowly, and the background moves slowest. The same relative movement occurs when the camera dollies out.

Crane up and down

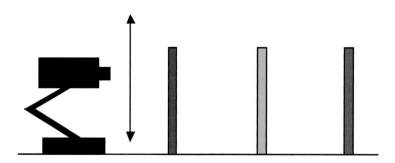

Camera moves up or down on a vertical axis also create relative movement.

 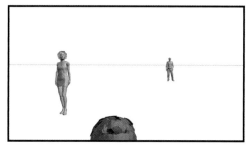

As the camera cranes up, the foreground moves fastest, the midground slower, and the background slowest. The audience sees the speed differences as a cue to depth.

4. Object Movement

In 3D, objects can actually move in depth along the Z-axis towards or away from the camera or audience.

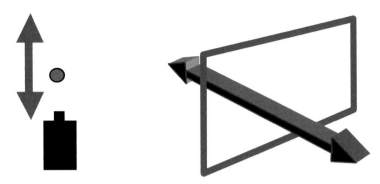

When an object of constant speed moves towards or away from the camera, the object's speed appears to change. As the object moves away, its movement slows; as an object moves closer, its speed increases. The audience perceives these apparent speed changes as depth. Additionally, Z-axis object movement activates other depth cues, including size and textural change, which are discussed later in this section.

5. Perspective and Converging Lines

Perspective is an important visual tool for creating depth.

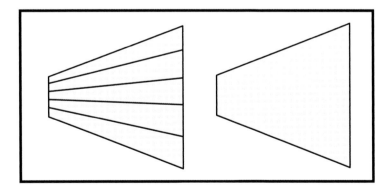

Any plane surface (like walls, floors, ceilings) can be used to create perspective, but it's the converging lines that add the depth. The two planes pictured above are identical but the one with more converging lines appears to have more depth.

For the purposes of creating depth, perspective can be divided into three categories: one-, two-, and three-point perspective.

Here are pictures of one-, two-, and three-point perspective, each with diagrams revealing the convergence. Generally, the apparent depth expands as the number of vanishing points increases, although it's very difficult for an audience to sense additional depth beyond three points.

6. Textural Diffusion

Objects with more textural detail seem closer and objects with less detail appear farther away.

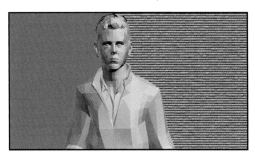

The wall on the right with more texture appears closer than the texture-less wall on the left. 3D's depth can be heightened by adding texture or detail to foreground objects and removing it from background objects.

Objects without any texture or vertical detail, like a perfectly smooth wall surface, a pitch black night sky, or an overexposed, white daytime sky, can be a problem. These objects won't generate an image pair with volume or vertical parallax. No matter where you try to place texture-less objects in depth, they will always move to the ZPS or screen plane. Texture, detail, or patterns with verticals are needed to create parallax. See Appendix E for a demonstration of this important principle.

7. Size Difference

A larger object looks closer and a smaller object seems farther away.

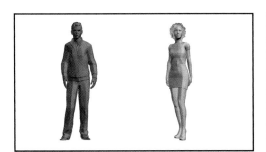 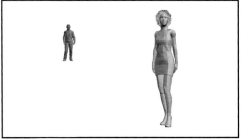

Size change seems to be an obvious depth cue, but the staging of objects along the Z-axis is critical to creating depth.

In 2D pictures, size change is an extremely important depth cue for staging a scene but also for backings and visual effects. In 3D, small-scale scenery built to appear farther away will be exposed as miniatures.

8. Tonal Separation

Generally, brighter objects seem closer and darker objects seem farther away.

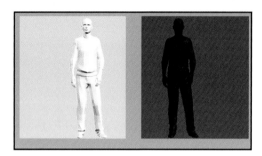

In 3D, lighting can be used to enhance object volume and position along the Z-axis. Fill light in 3D is required to keep objects from being completely underexposed, which makes it impossible to photograph an image pair. It is possible to reverse the tonal separation cue using aerial diffusion (discussed below).

9. Color Separation

Color separation is similar to tonal separation but refers to the hue of an object not its brightness.

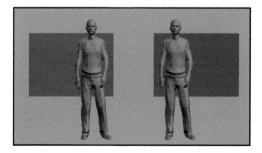

Warmer hues (red, orange, yellow) appear closer and cooler hues (green, blue) appear farther away. This principle does not always work because so many other depth cues can override the color separation but, all things being equal, warmer colors tend to advance and cooler colors tend to recede. This is particularly critical in production design and lighting.

10. Up/Down Position

The height placement of objects will affect their perceived depth.

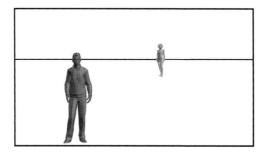

The red actor looks closer and the green actor seems farther away. Objects have a curious relationship to their height in the frame and the horizon line. When objects are below the horizon line, lower is closer and higher is farther away. But it flips when working above the horizon line, so lower seems farther away and higher is closer. The above example also uses size and color to enhance the depth.

11. Aerial diffusion

Particles suspended in the air (smog, fog, smoke, dust, rain) can affect the apparent depth because aerial diffusion affects other depth cues. Aerial diffusion prematurely reduces textural detail in the background so objects seem even farther away. Aerial diffusion also reduces tonal contrast and changes the color of objects to the color of the aerial diffusion.

In this illustration, the aerial diffusion is gray fog. As the fog's density increases, more of the shot is affected. There are still strong tonal contrasts in the foreground but the background has very little contrast or detail due to the fog. Finally, the gray fog has overwhelmed the background colors and turned them to the color of the gray fog. The fog pushes the background farther away, giving the shot more depth. A denser fog could push the midground and even the foreground away from the viewer.

In daylight, aerial diffusion turns backgrounds lighter, which contradicts the depth cue of tonal separation. At night, depending on the lighting, the aerial diffusion may darken the background.

12. Shape Constancy

Depth is enhanced when the shape silhouette of an object changes by turning in three-dimensional space or having the camera rotate around it.

As this car turns, its shape changes from a long rectangle to a square. The shape change is a cue to three-dimensional depth. Some objects, like a ball, don't change shape when they rotate. That lack of shape change doesn't make the ball less spherical, but it does eliminate an important cue that we use to judge an object's three-dimensionality.

When objects in a 3D movie lack volume, their shape changes may look odd because they seem to morph from one 2D shape to another.

13. Overlap

Although this is a minor depth cue, the depth is enhanced when an object overlaps or appears in front of or behind another object.

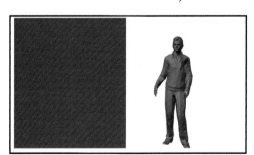 

When the actor stands partially behind the wall, the overlap adds depth.

Understanding the Depth Bracket and the depth cues are critical to creating three-dimensional depth. Both of these photos have the same Depth Bracket. But the grocery store aisle photo, which utilizes all the traditional depth cues, appears much deeper. We are so accustomed to using 2D depth cues to perceive depth that they appear to add even more depth to a 3D shot. In 3D, it can be misleading to rely only on the Depth Bracket as a measure of the apparent depth in a scene.

14. Depth-of-Field

Depth-of-field refers to the area along the Z-axis that is in acceptably sharp focus.

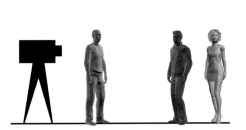 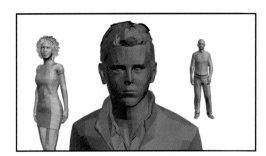

Deep focus or large depth-of-field

Deep focus or a **large depth-of-field** means that most, or all of a scene is in focus. In the above illustration, all three actors are in sharp focus. Because of the way our eyes and brain work, real-life human vision appears to have a constant, large depth-of-field in almost all viewing circumstances.

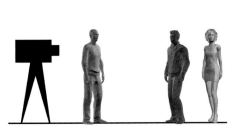 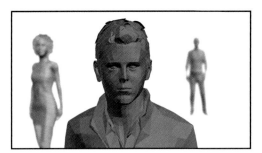

Shallow depth-of-field

A **shallow depth-of-field** means that only a small area of a scene is in focus. In this illustration, only the foreground actor is in sharp focus. Shallow depth-of-field is really an invention of photography because human vision generally maintains deep focus.

In 3D, it's not always necessary to mimic human vision and maintain deep focus but it's a good place to start. Even blurred foregrounds and backgrounds usually preserve their image pair parallax that places them in Z-axis depth. But a shallow depth-of-field may also reduce the effectiveness of other depth cues. Out-of-focus objects can lose their textural detail, size, or shape characteristics, which visually contribute to the apparent depth of the scene.

Depth-of-field is a visual style choice for filmmakers. Although 3D usually reveals more depth when everything is in sharp focus, blurry foregrounds or backgrounds are visual styles that can be explored.

Controlling depth-of-field in 3D has two purposes:

1. Separating the foreground, midground, and background.
2. Controlling directorial emphasis.

1. Depth-of-field separates the FG, MG, and BG

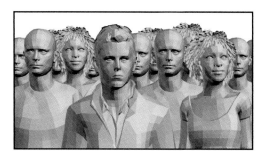

In 2D, the crowd blends together. It may have depth, but 2D photography struggles to record it.

A 2D shallow depth-of-field separates the foreground actor from the midground and background crowd. This tends to create depth, but the midground and background still merge together into a single plane without any depth.

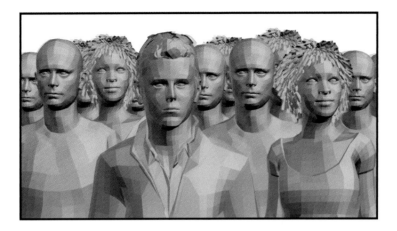

Put on your 3D glasses. The same shot separates into a foreground, midground, and background with depth. The depth is preserved in 3D without the help of a shallow depth-of-field.

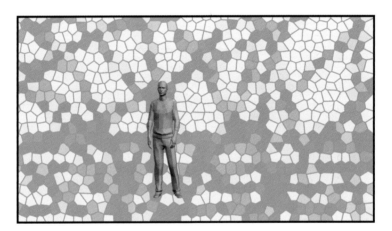

In 2D, a complex or heavily textured background can camouflage foreground subjects and make them difficult to see.

Blurring the background separates the foreground subject.

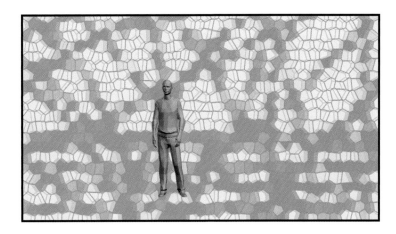

In 3D, the foreground subject can be separated from the background using Z-axis depth.

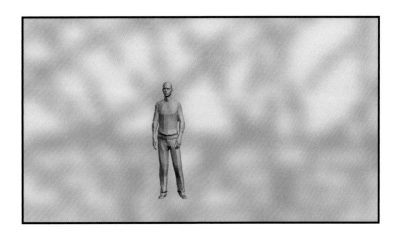

The background can also be blurred because it usually retains its image pair and a discernable parallax that places it in Z-axis depth.

2. Depth-of-field controls directorial emphasis

In 2D, the audience's attention will usually be drawn to the subject in focus. A good director or cinematographer can use selective focus to lead the audience's point-of-attention to the subject. Even though the foreground actor dominates the composition, the background actor in sharp focus commands your attention.

The same shot in 3D can have a different effect.

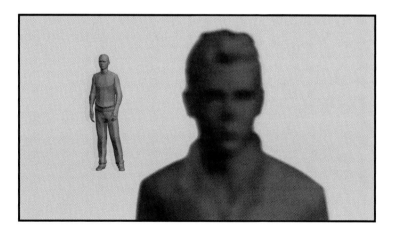

In 3D, the audience's point-of-attention is not as easily controlled by lens focus because the audience involuntarily looks first at the object closest to it, even if it's blurry.

In 2D, a rack focus from the foreground to the background will automatically move the audience's point-of-attention to the in-focus object.

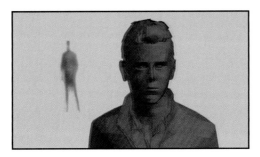 

In 3D this may not happen because the audience looks at foreground objects first. Additional visual techniques (such as darkening foreground objects) may be needed to direct the audience's attention elsewhere in the scene.

Closed and Open Space

2D Closed Space

Traditional 2D movies are almost entirely closed space.

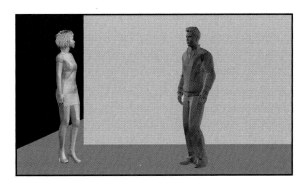

Closed space refers to the relationship between the picture and the frame lines that surround it. The frame lines are visually very strong. They surround the picture and clearly mark the border or edge of the picture itself. The picture only exists inside the frame, never outside of it. Viewers are always aware of the frame's edge and the fact that the picture is confined or closed in by the frame lines.

2D Open Space

Open space is difficult, but possible, to achieve in traditional 2D movies. Open space may occur when the movement within the frame is visually stronger than the frame lines. This movement overwhelms the frame lines and momentarily gives the audience the sense of visual space outside of the frame. A good example of 2D open space occurs at the beginning of *Star Wars Episode IV* (1976). As the enormous Imperial Destroyer spaceship flies into frame, most audience members look above the frame (often at the ceiling of the theatre) to see if the spaceship is overhead. Of course, it can't be anywhere but on the screen yet audiences feel the space has opened beyond the frame lines.

IMAX movies, because of the giant screen, can easily create open space. The screen is so large that the frame lines are beyond the audience's peripheral vision. Without frame lines or masking to close the space, the audience experiences open space. The ability to create open space diminishes as the screen size shrinks. Computer screens and handheld video devices can't open the space because the image is too small and the frame is too dominant.

Because open space occurs so rarely in 2D, it has unusual effects on the audience. Generally, it gives them a visual jolt. Open space in 2D attempts to mimic 3D's Personal Space experience.

3D Open Space

3D promotes open space because it exploits the space in front of (and behind) the screen. Audiences usually interpret objects in 3D Personal Space as open space.

There are several ways to create open space in 3D. View these examples with your 3D glasses.

1. An uncropped subject appearing in Personal Space creates open space. 3D movies with floating subjects can capitalize on this technique. The subject appears to have "escaped" the window plane.

2. A less effective open space occurs when the bottom of the window crops the subject. The subject still exists in the Personal Space in front of the window, but the bottom frame line crop begins to close the space. As any cropping increases, the possibility for creating open space diminishes.

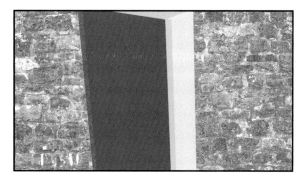

3. With the bottom and top of the subject cropped by the window, the open space's effectiveness is reduced even more.

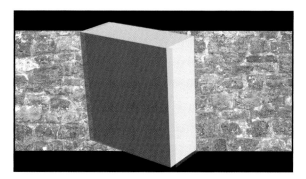

4. Open space is created when the Stereoscopic Window itself creates an artificial frame, which is actually part of the stereoscopic pair but appears to be part of the frame line. It's a visual trick. Objects can appear to overlap the window itself. This careful combination of a floating object and an artificial window creates the most effective open space.

3D Unstable Space

Uncorrected vertical window violations will cause the audience's visual field to become agitated. This can create an unstable feeling similar to camera-shake or unsteady handheld shots. Sometimes unstable space is described as weakening the frame lines, removing the barrier of the frame, or "letting the subject out of the box." Unstable space won't become open space but the frame can be made to feel visually agitated.

Unstable space occurs when vertical edge violations remain uncorrected. These violations can be caused by stationary objects along the frame's vertical edges, or by moving objects that quickly enter and exit the frame. Tiny non-subject violations won't create unstable space. The violations must be large enough and continue for enough time to destabilize the frame.

An action sequence may create unstable space when moving foreground objects constantly creates changing window violations. Camera compositions that purposely produce retinal rivalry can make the audience aware of the vertical frame lines and create an agitating, unstable space.

Unstable space can communicate a variety of emotions. Its visual agitation can make an audience feel unsafe or nervous, for example. Since unstable space may, over time, create eyestrain, it must be used carefully.

Pre-Visualizing 3D

Pre-visualization is a useful way to solve all kinds of problems prior to production. Story-boarding in 3D can be aided by color.

The color indicates three levels of depth. Red = foreground; yellow = ZPS; blue = background. The false color can be used to remind the filmmakers how much depth is required for a scene.

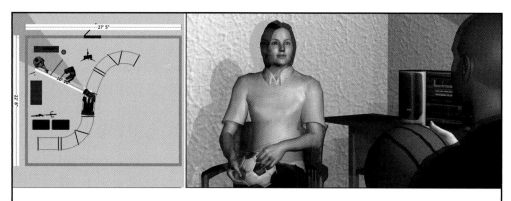

25-C M.S. Two Shot Over Albert's Shoulder

Maria fiddles nervously with the soccer ball as Albert exuberantly explains how he'd won the game. But both of them know full well that what's going on between them has nothing to do with what they're talking about. Maria hugs the soccer ball tight to her lap, a small shield between herself and Albert.

Camera Height: 3' 10"		Focal Length: 43.9mm		Angle of View: 27°
Roll: 0° | Tilt: -4.4° | HIT: 7.70%	|	Interaxial: 62mm | Screen Plane Dist: 5' 7"	|	Dist to Max Offset: 7' 5"

Previsualization by FrameForge Previz Studio
www.frameforge3d.com

Pre-visualization computer programs exist that allow you to build virtual sets, actors, and cameras in a 3D environment. You can move through the virtual environments and predetermine compositions, lens focal length, interaxial distances, Depth Brackets, and convergence points.

Pre-visualization engages 3D thinking early in the preparation of a production. It is important that your production team does not think in 2D and assume the 3D can be added later. 3D can only enhance the depth that is already there.

There is also a wide array of 3D calculators, computer programs, and apps that can be used to calculate your 3D camera settings. These programs offer a variety of approaches to help the cinematographer and production crew create 3D that is satisfying and comfortable to watch.

Visual Structure

Well-made movies and television shows have a visual design, a specific Movie-Suitcase, which controls the choices of staging, composition, color, lighting, and locations. 3D is another one of these visual design elements.

Adding 3D to a production can, like any other visual design element, be a simple or complex process. Take color, for example. Some directors, cinematographers, and production designers reduce their color palette to a single hue, like blue. Horror films are often based on an all-blue color scheme. A single, constant choice can also be made for 3D. An entire production can have a consistent amount of depth in every scene. The single color or the single 3D depth choice gives a production a specific visual style.

Production designer Richard Sylbert developed a more complex color palette for *Chinatown*. The plot involved municipal water rights, so as Sylbert described it, "everything was the color of plants that were dead from lack of water; blue and green only appeared if water was actually in the shot." An important part of the *Chinatown* visual style was due to Sylbert's ingenious color scheme. 3D can also be used in complex ways to underscore a theme, a character, a conflict, or a location.

To examine the relationship between story and 3D structures, we'll need a good story. The following examples use Alfred Hitchcock's *North By Northwest*. We're not suggesting that *North By Northwest* should be converted to 3D, although Hitchcock did use it for *Dial M for Murder*. The *North By Northwest* story structure is so strong that it makes an excellent template for any story discussion.

The following structural concepts are taken from the book *The Visual Story* by Bruce Block (Focal Press, 2008). In this book, they are applied to 3D filmmaking. There are three fundamental ways to link any aspect of visual structure to a story:

> **1. A Constant**
> **2. A Progression**
> **3. Contrast and Affinity.**

The CONSTANT is the simplest structure. It's a basic set of rules that are chosen, locked, and used for an entire production. *North by Northwest* is a compelling visual story. Any one of the following constant plans could be used to structure the 3D.

Here are three 3D constant plans:

CONSTANT PLAN 1: Conservative 3D
> CONVERGENCE: Subject Convergence (subject at ZPS).
> IA: Small Depth Bracket (+10 to -10 or 1 percent maximum).
> VOLUME: Off-model or less that 1:1.
> LENS: Moderate wide angle and normal lenses.
> STEREOSCOPIC WINDOW: Fixed at screen surface.

CONSTANT PLAN 2: Moderate 3D
> CONVERGENCE: Subject Convergence (subject at ZPS).
> IA: Medium Depth Bracket (+15 to –45 or 3 percent).
> VOLUME: On-model or 1:1.
> LENS: Wide angle.
> STEREOSCOPIC WINDOW: Mildly variable.

CONSTANT PLAN 3: Aggressive 3D
> CONVERGENCE: Shot Convergence.
> IA: Large Depth Bracket (+25 to –70 or about 5 percent).
> VOLUME: On-model or 1:1.
> LENS: Wide angle.
> STEREOSCOPIC WINDOW: Large position shifts.

Each of these three examples defines a set of consistent rules. Once the filmmakers decide if they want conservative or aggressive 3D, they can pick a plan and use it. It's a visual choice just like picking a color. Choosing a constant plan makes it easier for the filmmakers to work together because there's a set of visual rules. A constant also gives the finished production visual unity and if the constant choices are clever, the production can even look unique.

The PROGRESSION is the second basic choice for 3D structure and it's a more complex plan. The 3D progresses or migrates from one set of visual rules to another during the course of the story. In *North by Northwest*, the main character, Roger Thornhill (Cary Grant), gets progressively deeper into trouble and eventually must confront Vandamm (James Mason) and his thugs. As Thornhill's story conflict increases, the 3D parallels it and progressively grows in intensity.

PROGRESSION PLAN 1: A Depth Bracket change
>   CONVERGENCE: Subject Convergence (subject at ZPS).
>   IA: Small Depth Bracket (+5 to –5 or 0.5 percent)
>   PROGRESSES TO: Large Depth Bracket (+20 to –60 or 4 percent).
>   VOLUME: Reduced volume progresses to on-model or 1:1.
>   LENS: Moderate wide angle.
>   STEREOSCOPIC WINDOW: Fixed at screen surface.

The Depth Bracket progressively changes over the course of the story. It begins small (0.5 percent) and increases in size (4 percent). The story gains 3D depth as it unfolds. The climax of the story, at Mount Rushmore, will have the most Z-axis depth.

PROGRESSION PLAN 2: A convergence and Depth Bracket change
>   CONVERGENCE: Subject Convergence (subject at ZPS)
>   PROGRESSES TO: Shot Convergence (subject moves in depth)
>   IA: Small Depth Bracket (+5 to –5 or 0.5 percent)
>   PROGRESSES TO: Large Depth Bracket (+20 to –60 or 4 percent).
>   VOLUME: Reduced volume progresses to on-model or 1:1.
>   LENS: Moderate wide angle.
>   STEREOSCOPIC WINDOW: Fixed at screen surface.

In progression plan 2, the convergence changes and the Depth Bracket increase in size. The beginning of the story uses Subject Convergence. Thornhill, the subject, will remain at the ZPS no matter where he moves along the Z-axis. This lack of 3D movement is a correlate for Thornhill's predicament. He's a victim. As Thornhill takes charge of his situation, the 3D slowly shifts to Shot Convergence allowing Thornhill to move in Z-axis depth. Now Thornhill is more aggressive. The Depth Bracket also makes a progression from small to large. So the visual affect for the audience is that Thornhill's movement gains dynamic and depth as the story develops.

PROGRESSION PLAN 3: A convergence, Depth Bracket, and window change
>   CONVERGENCE: Subject Convergence (subject at ZPS)
>   PROGRESSES TO: Shot Convergence (subject moves in depth)
>   IA: Small Depth Bracket (+5 to -5 or 0.5 percent)
>   PROGRESSES TO: Large Depth Bracket (+20 to –60 or 4 percent).
>   VOLUME: Reduced volume progresses to on-model or 1:1.
>   LENS: Moderate wide angle.
>   STEREOSCOPIC WINDOW: Scenes appear in World Space
>   PROGRESSES TO: Scenes appear in Personal Space

This third plan includes the convergence and Depth Bracket progressions described in plan 2 but adds a progressive shift of the Depth Bracket and window positions. At the beginning of the story, the Depth Bracket is in the World Space behind the window. As the story evolves, the Depth Bracket moves in front of the window, the window moves back, and most of the depth plays in the Personal Space. As Thornhill becomes more involved with Eve Kendall (Eva Marie Saint), their story becomes more personal. This progressive 3D shift brings the visuals physically closer to the audience and makes the story more intimate and immersive. The Mt. Rushmore story climax can have the largest Depth Bracket and use the Personal and World Space to maximize the Z-axis depth.

The third type of 3D structure involves the critical visual concept: **_The Principle of Contrast and Affinity_**. This term requires some explanation. Contrast is defined as difference. Examples of visual contrast include: dark vs. light tones, warm vs. cool colors, vertical vs. horizontals lines. Affinity means similarity. Examples of visual affinity are: only darker tones, only cool colors, only horizontal lines.

The Principle of Contrast and Affinity states:

Visual Contrast adds intensity
and
Visual Affinity reduces intensity

This basic, universal principle is applied to painting, drawing, interior decoration, architecture, industrial design, sound, and movies. Of course, the Principle of Contrast and Affinity also applies to 3D.

Contrast in 3D includes:
>   Depth Bracket size: large vs. small
>   Convergence: Shot Convergence vs. Subject Convergence
>   Volume: 0 percent vs. 100 percent vs. 150 percent
>   Scene placement: World Space vs. Personal Space
>   Stereoscopic Window: moving vs. stationary

Affinity in 3D includes:
>   Depth Bracket size: doesn't change
>   Convergence: Shot Convergence or Subject Convergence but not both
>   Volume: doesn't change
>   Scene placement: World Space or Personal Space but not both
>   Stereoscopic Window: locked in one position

The more 3D contrast, the greater the visual intensity. The more affinity, the less visual intensity will be generated by the 3D. The Principle of Contrast and Affinity is the most useful tool for orchestrating the 3D visual structure in direct relationship to specifics in the story.

North By Northwest provides excellent opportunities to harness 3D to the Principle of Contrast and Affinity. Hitchcock has structured his story with rises and falls in dramatic intensity.

Here's a synopsis of the first 15 minutes of the story: Roger Thornhill is an advertising executive who's mistaken for a government agent. He's kidnapped, taken to a secluded mansion, drugged, and set off to die in a runaway car accident.

Hitchcock is already using the Principle of Contrast and Affinity in his 2D compositions, camera angles, and editorial rhythms. As Thornhill's conflict escalates, Hitchcock increases the visual contrast. A 3D visual structure can be designed to serve the same purpose. All of this leads to creating a 3D script that permits the filmmakers to plan the 3D from sequence to sequence in direct relation to the story.

The following 3D script outlines the first six story sequences in North By Northwest. This script also outlines three 3D variables:

1. A convergence plan. Will you use Subject Convergence where the subject of each shot stays at the ZPS or will you use Shot Convergence where the subject can move along the Z-axis getting closer or farther from the audience?
2. A Depth Bracket size. How big will the 'depth of the box' or the Depth Bracket be? Which scenes will use more Z-axis depth and which scenes will be shallow?
3. A placement of the Depth Bracket. Will a majority of the composition appear in the World Space behind the window or will it move in front of the window in the audience's Personal Space?

Story Sequence	Convergence Plan	Depth Bracket Size	Shot Placement
1. Thornhill is a busy executive	Subject	40 pixels, 2%	World Space
2. Thornhill is kidnapped	Subject	40 pixels, 2%	Personal Space
3. Vandamm at mansion library	Subject/shot	20 pixels, 1%	World Space
4. Drunk driving	Shot	85 pixels, 4.5%	Personal and World Space
5. Police station	Subject	40 pixels, 2%	World Space
6. Return to mansion library	Shot	40 pixels, 2%	Personal Space

The convergence plan uses Subject Convergence to keep the subject at the ZPS during sequences 1–3. Keeping the subject in the same place along the Z-axis creates affinity and lowers the visual intensity. At the end of sequence 3 when the bourbon is brought out, there's a shift to Shot Convergence. This creates visual contrast, which parallels the story intensity escalation. The bourbon signifies story intensity and so will the 3D convergence shift. The shift in convergence provides 3D contrast that creates visual intensity. The Shot Convergence continues through the drunk driving (sequence 4).

The Depth Bracket is kept small in sequences 1-3 until the drunk driving, where the bracket expands. This change is a good example of the Principle of Contrast and Affinity. By keeping the Depth Bracket small in sequence 3, its sudden size change in sequence 4 will be more intense. The drunk driving can also use unstable space or open space to create even more visual intensity.

The shot placement in sequence 1 is in World Space and shifts to Personal Space when the kidnapping occurs (sequence 2), making it more immersive and aggressive. The mansion library (sequence 3) returns to World Space to set up a visual contrast with the drunk driving (sequence 4). The drunk driving is a 3D rollercoaster ride and alternates between Personal Space and World Space, intensifying the audience's visual experience of Thornhill's perilous road trip. The police station (sequence 5) uses World Space but when Thornhill returns to the mansion library to prove his innocence (sequence 6), everything is the same while also suspiciously different. One difference is a change from World Space (sequence 3) to Personal Space (sequence 6).

On the next page is a 3D script of the middle section of *North By Northwest*.

Story Sequence	Convergence Plan	Depth Bracket Size	Shot Placement
7. Thornhill finds hotel room	Subject	40 pixels, 2%	World Space
8. United Nations waiting room	Subject/shot	60 pixels, 3%	Personal Space
9. Intelligence headquarters	Subject	30 pixels, 1.5%	World Space
10. Grand Central Station	Shot	40 pixels, 2%	World Space
11. Thornhill meets Kendall on train	Shot	40 pixels, 2%	Personal Space
12. Chicago train station	Shot	20 pixels, 1%	Personal Space
13. Crop duster	Shot	100 pixels, 5.25%	World and Personal Space
14. Chicago hotel room	Shot	40 pixels, 2%	Personal Space
15. Auction house bidding	Shot	60 pixels, 3%	Personal Space
16. The professor intervenes	Subject	40 pixels, 2%	Personal Space

The next important story sequence occurs at the United Nations building (sequence 8). Unexpectedly, a man is stabbed and Thornhill is blamed. His problem suddenly escalates from a nuisance drunk driving ticket to a murder. The 3D shifts to Shot Convergence and Personal Space when the stabbing occurs. Except for the two sequences with the professor (Sequences 9 and 16), the 3D plan uses Shot Convergence to give Thornhill more intense, dynamic movement along the Z-axis.

The Depth Bracket is larger at the United Nations but then becomes conservative until the crop duster scene (sequence 13) when it expands to 100 pixels.

The shot placement makes a shift towards more Personal Space as the story continues. The exception is the crop duster sequence, which uses both Personal and World Space to intensify the action.

Hitchcock constantly plays with the Principle of Contrast and Affinity. He cuts to an unusually extreme high shot looking down on the United Nations Plaza as Thornhill runs to a cab. The size contrast from the close-up stabbing to the extreme wide angle not only builds intensity but shows Thornhill as a tiny victim in an overwhelming environment. In 3D, the high shot could be further punctuated with an unusually large Depth Bracket.

Story Sequence	Convergence Plan	Depth Bracket Size	Shot Placement
17. Mt. Rushmore visitor center	Shot	60 pixels, 3%	Personal Space
18. Thornhill and Kendall reunite	Shot	40 pixels, 2%	Personal Space
19. Thornhill in hospital	Shot	40 pixels, 2%	Personal Space
20. Vandamm's house	Shot	60 pixels, 3%	World and Personal Space
21. Walk to Vandamm's plane	Shot	40 pixels, 2%	Personal Space
22. Mt. Rushmore sequence	Shot	100 pixels, 5.25%	World and Personal Space
23. Thornhill and Kendall on train	Shot	40 pixels, 2%	Personal Space

The final section of the *North By Northwest* 3D script uses Shot Convergence to add variety to the subject depth and create more visual contrast.

The Depth Bracket changes in size but becomes largest during the Mt. Rushmore chase.

The shot placement favors the Personal Space but both Personal and World Spaces are used to add intensity to Vandamm's house (sequence 20) and, of course, Mt. Rushmore (sequence 22).

The same 3D script concept can be used for a specific sequence. Here's a story beat breakdown for the crop duster sequence from *North By Northwest*. This classic ten minutes is a perfect example of a story intensity build.

Sequence Beats	Convergence Plan	Depth Bracket Size	Shot Placement
1. Thornhill arrives by bus	Subject	40 pixels, 2%	World Space
2. Thornhill waits at roadside	Subject	40 pixels, 2%	World Space
3. Man arrives and takes the bus	Subject	40 pixels, 2%	World Space
4. Plane attack #1	Transition to Shot Convergence	60 pixels, 3%	Personal Space
5. Plane attack #2 w/ machine gun	Shot	60 pixels, 3%	Personal Space
6. Thornhill tries to stop passing car	Shot	60 pixels, 3%	Personal Space
7. Plane attack #3 w/ machine gun	Shot	60 pixels, 3%	Personal Space
8. Plane attack #4	Shot	70 pixels, 3.5%	Personal Space
9. Plane attack #5 w/ chemicals	Shot	90 pixels, 4.5%	Personal Space
10. Plane hits truck and explodes	Shot	90 pixels, 4.5%	Personal Space
11. Thornhill steals truck and escapes	Shot	30 pixels, 1.5%	Transition to World Space

This depth script uses Subject Convergence until the plane attacks begin. All of the plane attacks use Shot Convergence so that Thornhill and the plane actually move towards the audience.

The Depth Bracket increases in size as the action develops. By the climax (the explosion in beat 10), the Depth Bracket has grown to 90 pixels or 4.5 percent.

The crop duster sequence begins in World Space and as the attacks intensify the action moves closer to the audience into the Personal Space. When Thornhill escapes in a stolen truck and the story intensity reduces, the shots move back into World Space.

The crop duster sequence could be given even more 3D intensity by exploiting the Principle of Contrast and Affinity. There is a lull in the plane attacks during beat #6 when Thornhill tries to stop a passing car. During that beat, the Depth Bracket could reduce in size and the scene could push back into the World Space. This reduction of the 3D dynamics parallels the decreased story conflict. By contrast, the plane resuming its attack (beat 7) will feel even more intense because it was preceded by less 3D in beat 6. This 3D plan is based on evaluating what Hitchcock did with his 2D visual structure and applying the same principles to the 3D variables.

Another system for planning and orchestrating the relationship between the story structure and any aspect of visual structure is by drawing graphs. In broad strokes, a story is an arrangement of scenes built around a conflict. The conflict can be based on an external situation (battling aliens, escaping prisoners, crime-fighting cops) or an internal struggle (heart-broken lovers, impassioned lawyers, bitter teenagers). Many stories combine external and internal conflicts together. Every story structure builds in intensity and pushes the conflict towards a climax and an ending resolution.

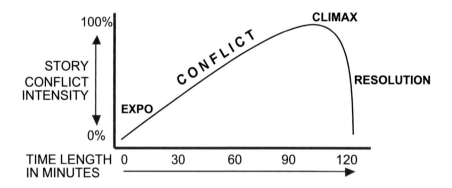

Any story structure can be plotted on a story graph. It lays out the build in the story conflict (from 0 percent intensity to 100 percent intensity) from the opening exposition through to the ending resolution. In this example, the story is measured in minutes along the bottom of the graph. But this graph is very general and doesn't reflect the specific changes in a story's structure.

Here the same basic graph has been adapted to *North By Northwest*. The story conflict's rises and falls are indicated by the height of the graph's red line.

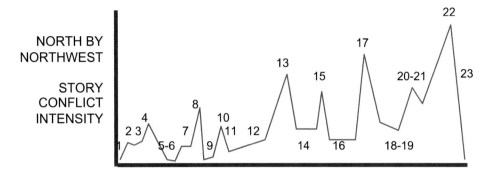

The numbers in the graph refer to the numbered sequences on the *North By Northwest* 3D script. This graph is very useful but perhaps too complex to easily read.

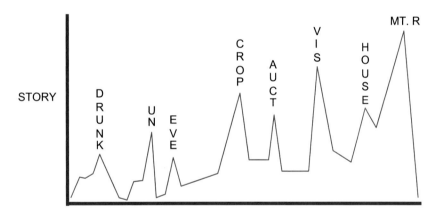

Here's a simpler version of the *North By Northwest* story graph with labels on the more intense story sequences:

Seq. 4: DRUNK (drunk driving)
Seq. 8: UN (United Nations stabbing)
Seq. 11: EVE (Thornhill meets Eve Kendall)
Seq. 13: CROP (crop duster)
Seq. 15: AUCT (art auction)
Seq. 17: VIS (Mt. Rushmore Visitor Center)
Seq. 20: HOUSE (Vandamm's house)
Seq. 22: MT. R (Mt. Rushmore chase)

The constant, progression, and Contrast and Affinity plans can be structured in relation to the story.

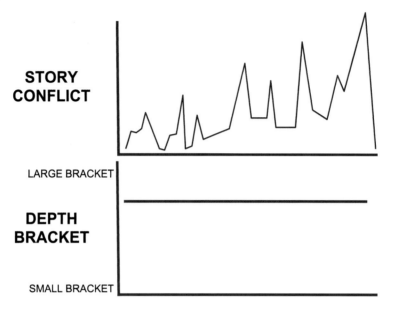

A second graph is placed directly below the story graph. In this case, the second graph indicates a 3D plan that uses a ***constant*** Depth Bracket size. The constant looks dull on a graph but looks can be deceiving. A carefully chosen constant can be a solid foundation for a 3D plan. Like a single color choice, an unchanging Depth Bracket can give a production visual unity. The "depth of the box" of your movie can have a single definition that makes it visually unique.

The Depth Bracket size should be controlled primarily by the staging and composition of the shots. The Depth Bracket can also be controlled by the camera's IA or lens focal length, but that may adversely affect volume.

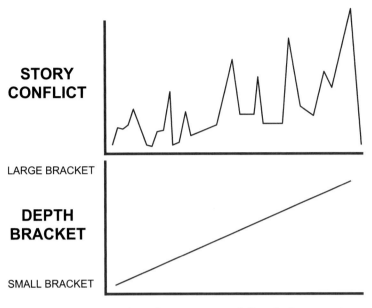

This 3D structure uses a ***progression***. If a constant is dull or lacks intensity, a progression may better suit your story. The Depth Bracket can expand as the story becomes more complex. This structure could also be reversed so the Depth Bracket is reduced as the story unfolds. You make this choice based on your story structure. In *North By Northwest*, Roger Thornhill's problems and the Depth Bracket size can increase simultaneously.

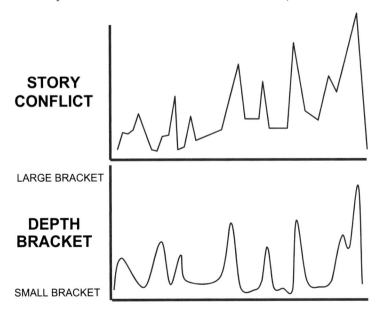

Here, the size of the Depth Bracket parallels the amount of conflict in the story. As the conflict intensifies, the Depth Bracket expands and when the conflict calms down, the Depth Bracket reduces in size. This is a common plan in action films.

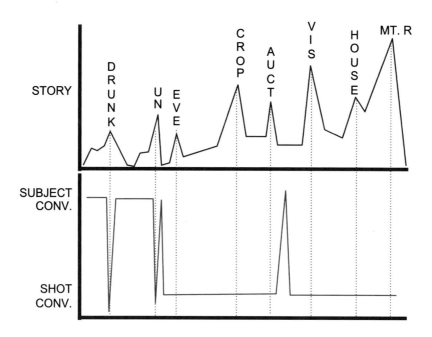

But you can get even more complex, specific, and creative. You can structure the depth as carefully as a composer orchestrates the music. This lower graph is a specific 3D plan for a scene-by-scene structure for Subject or Shot Convergence. To identify specific scenes, the story graph has labels of key scenes from *North By Northwest*.

The movie uses Subject Convergence and shifts to Shot Convergence for the drunk driving and the United Nations sequences. Once Thornhill meets Eve Kendall, the rest of the film (except for seq. 16 when the professor intervenes) uses Shot Convergence. Shot Convergence allows the subject to move on the Z-axis towards and away from the viewer. This kind of Z-axis movement can add intensity to action sequences.

Aligning the second graph directly under the story graph relates the visual decisions directly to a specific scene in the story. This creates an important relationship between the two structures that can be planned and easily changed.

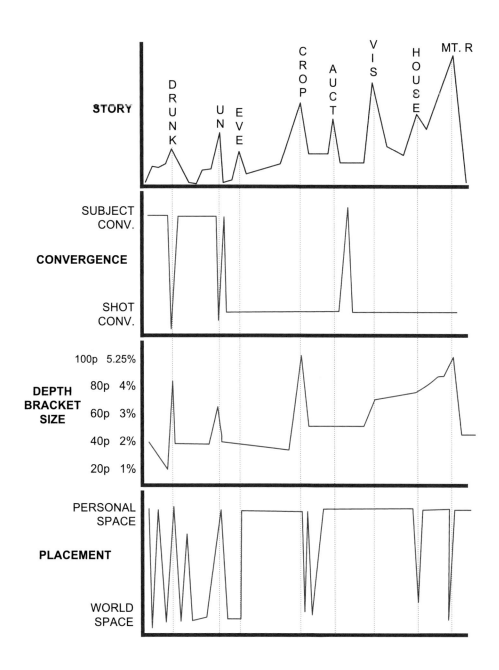

Three graphs have been added under the *North By Northwest* story graph. They indicate the 3D structure for the convergence, Depth Bracket size, and shot placement in World or Personal Space. These visual variables become part of the storytelling. The Principle of Contrast and Affinity is the control that can help you ramp up the intensity or reduce it to fit the story.

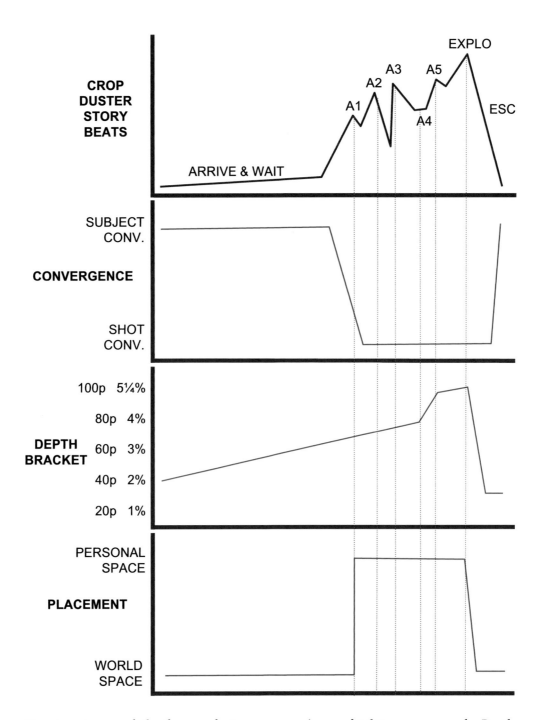

Here is a story graph for the crop duster sequence plus graphs for convergence, the Depth Bracket, and the shot placement. The story beats indicate Thornhill's arrival and wait, the plane attacks (A1 through A5), the explosion, and Thornhill's escape. Each 3D variable is planned to support the story's intensity build.

The Depth Bracket can be orchestrated within a single shot to parallel the story conflict. This example is taken from a single continuous shot in *How to Train Your Dragon*. In this scene, Hiccup (the boy) sees Toothless (the dragon) for the first time. It is the critical beginning of their relationship.

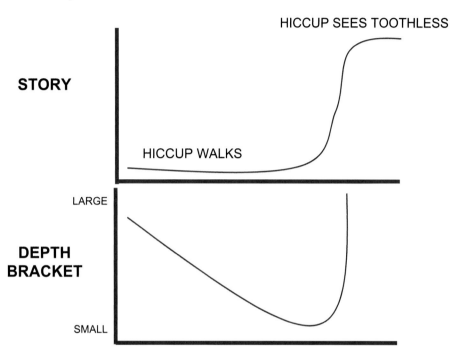

The story graph indicates Hiccup's action as he walks nervously through the forest, anxiously peers over a hill and sees Toothless right in front of him. The dramatic tension starts low but jumps up quickly when the boy sees the dragon.

The shot's 3D, in the lower graph, is designed to parallel the story intensity. The shot begins with a large Depth Bracket. As Hiccup walks through the forest, the Depth Bracket slowly reduces, leaving the shot without much 3D depth. As Hiccup peeks over a hill and sees the dragon, the Depth Bracket dramatically expands. This sudden change in 3D depth emphasizes Hiccup's adrenalin rush. The Principle of Contrast and Affinity in conjunction with the Depth Bracket has intensified an important moment in the story.

Later, in the same sequence, Hiccup is poised, ready to stab Toothless. Hiccup stands over the dragon with his knife raised, gathering the courage to strike. No matter how he struggles, Hiccup is a pacifist at heart. He relents and the dramatic tension is released.

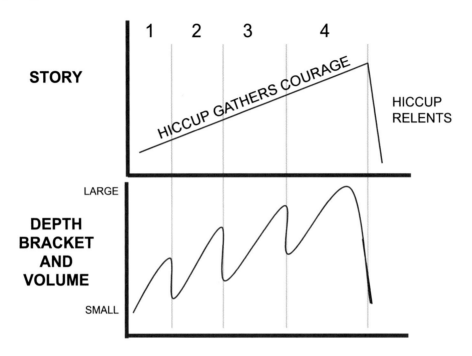

The story graph diagrams this brief sequence. There are four shots of Hiccup. In each shot, the Depth Bracket starts small and grows larger in size as Hiccup struggles with his inner conflict as a reluctant warrior.

Ultimately, Hiccup can't kill the dragon and he drops the knife. The Depth Bracket drops back to a smaller size. The Depth Bracket dimension is directly tied to Hiccup's emotional build up and release. The 3D visual and story structures are working in parallel.

In the animated feature film *Puss In Boots* (2011), a beat-by-beat 3D plan was designed to parallel a three-minute sequence in the story.

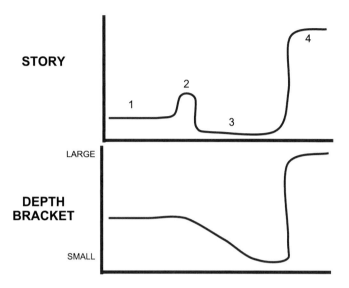

The upper graph diagrams the story sequence's four beats: (1) Puss, Kitty, and Humpty walk through the desert and plant the magic beans; (2) a foreboding storm overwhelms the group; (3) a tiny plant sprouts and the disappointed threesome wait; (4) suddenly the beanstalk erupts with growth and pulls everyone skyward.

The lower graph diagrams the size of the Depth Bracket. Placing the Depth Bracket graph under the story graph allows the relationship between the two structures to be seen clearly. The Depth Bracket changes occur in parallel with the intensity of the story action.

Beat 1: The Depth Bracket is moderate as the characters enter and plant the beans.

Beat 2: Although the momentary storm is foreboding, the 3D depth remains moderate. The brief storm tricks the audience into thinking the beanstalk is out of control. There is also some unstable space to give the storm some visual intensity.

Beat 3: As the characters stand over the tiny bean plant, the Depth Bracket and volume slowly reduce to zero. Almost all of the 3D depth and volume drain from the shot. Visually, the shot has lost its intensity.

Beat 4: The plant explodes and rapidly grows. The Depth Bracket suddenly expands to 150 pixels or about 8 percent and the volume returns. This Z-axis movement is extremely intense compared to the lack of movement, volume, and depth in beat 3. This is the Principle of Contrast and Affinity at work. These contrasts from shot to shot make the growing beanstalk extremely aggressive.

The 3D can be assigned to aspects of the story other than the conflict. The following examples do not refer to a particular film.

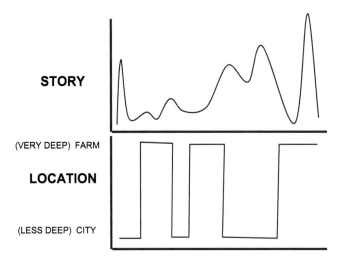

This story jumps back and forth between a large city and a farm. The amount of 3D depth can visually differentiate the two locations. The farm will use a large Depth Bracket and the city uses a small Depth Bracket.

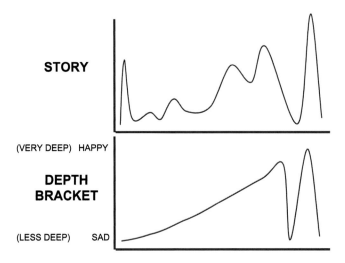

Here, the amount of 3D depth is associated with emotional happiness. As the main character becomes happy, the depth increases; as the character saddens, the depth decreases.

Assigning a meaning to 3D is the first step in structuring this important visual component. Even an unchanging, consistent amount of 3D depth will have an effect on the visual structure and the audience. Defining how the 3D space will be used makes directorial and design decisions easier and gives the audience a more interesting visual experience.

3D can be used as a visual correlate for any changes in moods, emotions, ideas, or locations. Here are some examples:

More 3D		**Less 3D**
Happy	vs.	Sad
Alone	vs.	United
Scary	vs.	Friendly
Real	vs.	Imaginary
Exteriors	vs.	Interiors
Good	vs.	Evil
Peace	vs.	War
Human	vs.	Animal
Chaos	vs.	Order

This list is completely arbitrary. The More/Less headings can be flipped to represent the opposite mood, emotion, idea, or location. It's up to the filmmaker to attach a specific purpose to the 3D and consistently use it in a production.

The position of the Depth Bracket can be used for dramatic emphasis.

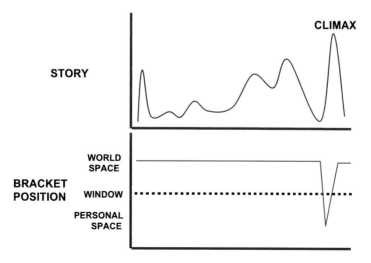

In this example, the Depth Bracket position begins in the World Space behind a stationary window. At the story climax, the Depth Bracket moves in front of the window into the Personal Space. This shift adds immersion and intensity to the climax of the story.

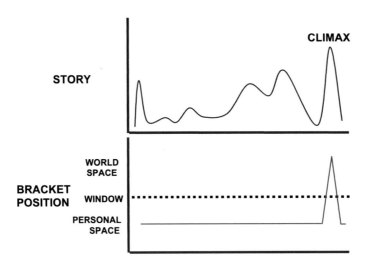

The same plan can be flipped. During the climax, the Depth Bracket moves from the Personal Space to the World Space. The general effect of this Depth Bracket shift may not have the same intensity as the previous example. The audience will feel a sense of the scene pulling away or becoming less immersive.

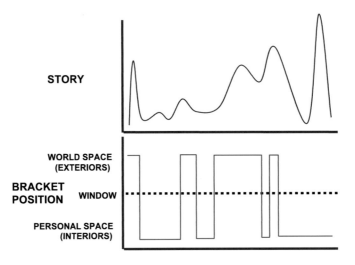

In this example, the Depth Bracket position indicates location. The World Space is used for exteriors and the Personal Space is used for interiors. The Stereoscopic Window remains stationary.

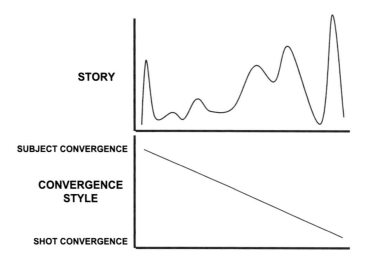

The graphs can be used to plan the style of convergence. The decision to use a progressive change from Subject Convergence to Shot Convergence is based on the story. This story conflict is about a reluctant fellow who's afraid to take action (like Hamlet). As he gains strength, the type of convergence shifts from keeping him at the screen plane to allowing him to move around in Z-axis depth. This 3D visual concept may sound overly complex or difficult for the audience to notice but filmmakers have been doing the same thing with composition, color, lighting, and movement for over 100 years.

Please see Appendix A to read personal accounts by stereographers and 3D supervisors discussing how they use 3D in their work.

Window and Camera Movement

The Stereoscopic Window's movement is limited to "in and out" or towards and away from the audience. The window can move during a shot or on the edit from shot-to-shot. Audiences are generally unaware of the window moving, especially when it's linked to camera or object movement.

Window movement can shift objects behind or in front of the window.

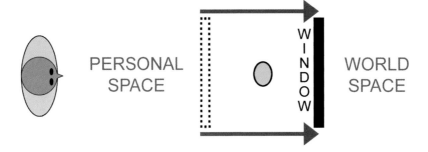

In this example, the object begins in World Space behind the window. As the window moves away from the audience (indicated by the red arrows), the object will pass through the window into the Personal Space. Window movement away from the audience that shifts an object out of World Space and into Personal Space usually increases the visual intensity.

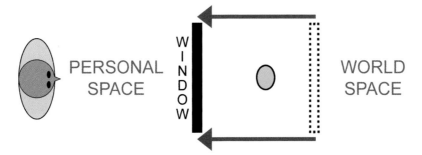

A moving window that shifts an object from Personal Space to World Space is usually less intense. As window movement slows down, it loses visual intensity. As window movement increases in speed, its visual intensity becomes greater.

The visual intensity of a shot may change when window movement is added to a camera move. Different combinations of these two movements allow the filmmaker to increase or reduce the visual intensity of a shot.

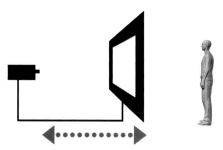

The camera and the window can be locked together and moved (in either direction) the same distance in the same amount of time. When locked to the camera movement, the window is a passive partner and has no effect on the intensity created by the camera movement.

When the window moves in the opposite direction of the camera, the intensity of the camera movement is reduced.

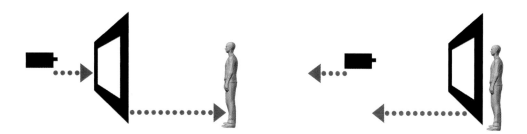

The intensity of the camera move is increased when it is combined with a window move in the same direction that goes farther and faster in the same amount of time.

3D and Editing

3D can have an affect on the apparent rhythm of traditional editing techniques. Some film-makers believe that you can't use fast cutting in 3D. You can, of course. It was believed that fast cutting caused eyestrain but these problems were often due to errors in 3D photography and projection. Fast cutting is not a problem in 3D if the filmmakers know what they're doing, but quick cutting will reduce the sense of depth during a sequence. There are two aspects of 3D that must be understood to use fast cutting properly.

> 1. Z-axis point of attention jumps.
> 2. Audience viewing time.

1. Z-axis jumps in the audience's point-of-attention from shot-to-shot usually make editorial rhythm seem faster. As the distance of the Z-axis subject jumps increase from shot-to-shot, the editorial pace seems to increase, too. As the Z-axis subject jump distance is reduced from shot-to-shot, the rhythm of the edited shots seems to return to the same pace as traditional 2D edits.

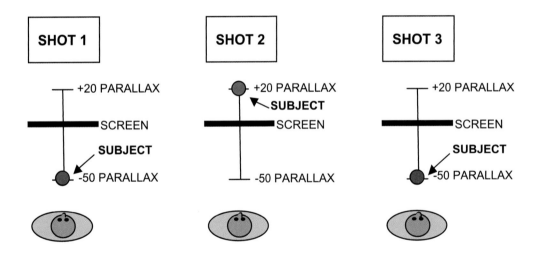

In this 3D editing situation, on the cut to incoming shots 2 and 3, the audience will have to jump their point-of-attention along the Z-axis to find the new subject. These subject jumps in Z-axis point-of-attention will make the editing pace seem faster. Point-of-attention is discussed in detail on pages 89–110.

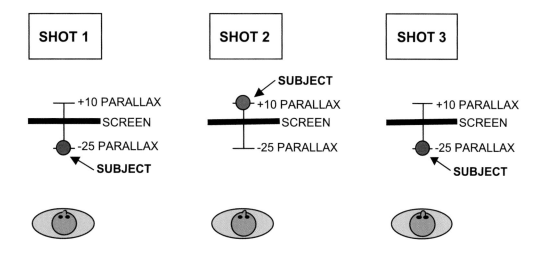

This is an adjusted version of the three shots. The point-of-attention subject jumps have been reduced due to restaging, IA changes, convergence adjustments, or postproduction manipulation. The perceived pace of the editorial rhythm will be less affected by these smaller Z-axis subject jumps.

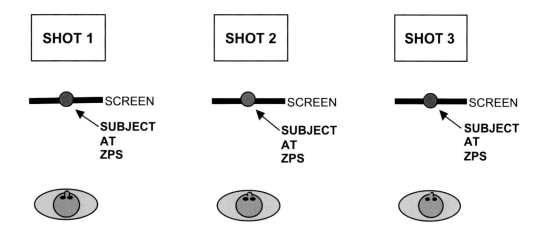

In this third version, the point-of-attention jumps have been completely eliminated due to restaging, IA changes, convergence adjustments, or postproduction manipulation. Now, the pace of the editorial rhythm will be unaffected by the subject's depth. Although the editorial rhythm is unaffected, the potential for interesting 3D subject depth is eliminated. Peripheral non-subject depth becomes essential to keeping the 3D alive.

2. The length of time the audience needs to acclimate to a shot can be longer in 3D than in traditional 2D. Dr. Tim J. Smith at the University of London made a series of visual tests to determine how audiences view the same shots in 2D and 3D. His results show that an audience can need from 0.5 to 2 seconds longer to examine a shot in 3D and find the subject. In fast editing, even if the subjects of each shot are without Z-axis jumps from shot-to-shot, the audience may miss visual information because they haven't had time to acclimate to the shot.

When a new 3D shot appears on screen, the audience's first instinct is to look at the object closest to them. If that closest object isn't the subject (as in an over-the-shoulder shot) the audience searches the shot on the X-, Y-, and Z-axis, which takes longer than a simple X- and Y-axis search in 2D. If the audience isn't given a little extra time in 3D to find the subject, they can miss important visual information. Even with adjustments made in the pace for 3D viewing, the audience may feel that the 3D editorial pace is too fast.

Evaluating 3D footage during editing is important. When editing in 3D, it is best to edit with a viewable 3D image, not a single left or right eye image. If the editor only views 3D scenes in 2D, footage with stereoscopic errors can go undetected.

Editorial rhythm in 2D or 3D is subjective so screening edited sequences in 3D is absolutely necessary. 3D should be viewed often, more often than traditional 2D productions. Of course, 3D must be viewed on a screen size as similar as possible to the screen size for which it was intended. Don't preview 3D footage designed for a 40-foot movie screen on a small TV monitor or 10-foot preview theatre screen. Undersized viewing situations will diminish the 3D effect, which will become surprisingly exaggerated on a 40-foot screen.

The more people who review the 3D, the more a filmmaker will learn about the limitations of parallax and the visual fatigue it can create. The key question is: how stressful is the parallax setting for the subject (the object you want the audience to look at)? A director, cinematographer, and production designer unfamiliar with 3D should make tests and view them on a proper size screen to determine what works best for their aesthetics, the story, and the technical limitations of their equipment. Key crew members need to have the common experience of seeing what works for them in 3D. No matter how accomplished you may be in your field, 3D is a new world and creating pictures using its visual grammar requires practice. Its absolutely critical for everyone involved to develop their skills and a visual language that takes advantage of the possibilities of spatial movie-making.

APPENDICES

APPENDIX A
STEREOGRAPHER INTERVIEWS

We asked a group of stereographers and 3D supervisors to talk about their work. Here are their thoughts about their 3D production experience.

ERIC DEREN has been working as a VFX and animation professional since 1993, has operated Dzignlight Studios since 1996, and has been working with stereoscopic 3D professionally since 1999. His breakout moment was a 2007 live-action stereoscopic aerial skydiving short, achieved years before the advent of small, off-the-shelf, synchronized stereoscopic cameras. In addition, Deren built a facility of 85 artists to support the 3D conversion of part of James Cameron's *Titanic*, is an accomplished camera operator, and builds motion control systems for 3D time lapse projects.

Deren writes:
Over the past years I have worked on many different kinds of productions. My technical approach to the 3D in these films was generally the same; however the role I played during production was radically different from film to film.

For example, on *Hidden 3D*, I was fully in charge of the 3D plan and execution. This particular production needed someone to come in and create a foundational plan for what kind of 3D we would be shooting, then roll up their sleeves and make the stereo camera system do exactly what it needed to do to capture that plan. I was fortunate to have this opportunity as my first stereoscopic feature film, and to have a director of photography, Benoit Beaulieu, who supported my decisions and me. My general plan was to capture natural volume as much as was possible, hiding most IA changes in camera movements. My general thoughts going into this film was that 3D should be like good sound FX or good VFX ... if the audience notices what was done, it was probably excessive. Even with this idea, I still executed a number of IA changes to accentuate uneasy or psychologically dynamic sequences. Though this was a lower-budget feature, there were still over 300 VFX shots in it, so care had to be taken in many shots to leave sufficient depth for CG elements that would be added later.

For the animated feature *Gnomeo and Juliet*, my job was to interact with our director, Kelly Asbury, and develop a plan that supported his vision for the film. I then supervised the execution of that plan, all the way through finishing to the DCP. This project, unlike *Hidden*, was more political in nature. Once I developed my plan, I had to nearly "sell" that plan to the production, explaining my plan in terms of the story that everyone was very familiar with. I did this using a visual "depth script" presentation document that I had developed after meeting with Phil McNally at DreamWorks. I used this document to demonstrate a reserved use of 3D during dramatic sequences and a stronger use of 3D during the action sequences, although we sometimes ended up straying from this plan due to technicalities of the existing film. *Gnomeo and Juliet* was interesting in that most of the 2D movie was completed by the time the decision was made to release it in 3D. This put the production in an interesting technical and creative position. Technically, the most time-efficient way to get a 3D version of this movie to the theaters was to take the existing renders and re-composite every shot in the film, doing 2D pixel offsets based on Z-depth to create an accurate second-eye view of every 2D composited element. Although this process worked well in most situations, we were given a budget for stereoscopically re-rendering a small percentage of shots in 3D for situations where this pixel-offset technique would not achieve satisfactory results.

Creatively, Mr. Asbury had a very clear vision of what he wanted to see in his movie and from the beginning he had wanted to tell this story with 3D. When I offered recommendations for alterations to his vision, he was very willing to have discussions about my recommendations, and would often defer to my judgment based on the strength of the case I was able to make.

Given Mr. Asbury's intent to tell the story with imagery, we were able to take advantage of the production's technical re-render capabilities, and we went back into layout for many shots to make them more conducive to 3D presentation. As such, a number of the shots in the 3D version of the film are significantly different from their 2D counterparts.

The Amazing Spider-Man was completely different from any of the previous films I had worked on. On this show, I executed a plan that was already in place, set forth by the production. This plan was to orchestrate the overall 3D depth during the course of the film, keeping depth shallow and very nearly 2D during dialogue sequences, and increasing the volumes during the action sequences, building to a celebration of 3D during the third-act climax. I had done this sort of "depth scripting" on previous projects, but never to the amount that had been set forth for *Spider-Man*. It was actually a great experience, not executing a 3D plan that I had designed, but executing a plan that someone else had designed. It was not unlike painting in the style of another artist, and it was a very technical experience. Audiences' reactions to the 3D approach of *Spider-Man* were very polarized, and it was interesting to see how viewers were split between rave reviews of the movie's 3D technique, and sanctimonious shouts of 3D blasphemy, as if the inclusion of a significant number of subtle 3D moments was an affront to some "correct" way to create 3D artistry.

On *Oz: The Great and Powerful*, I came in as a replacement for the first unit stereographer on several weeks of additional shooting. My job was to match what the stereographer on principal photography, James Goldman, had done. At first glance, this sounds like another technical study, but as it would turn out, after reviewing the imagery captured during principal, it became clear that Mr. Goldman and I have very similar stereoscopic styles and I found that my intuitive depth decisions were mirroring his almost exactly to the millimeter of IA. The overall feel of the 3D in this show achieved natural volumes, with a handful of fun 3D moments reflecting Sam Raimi's vision for the film. Our cinematographer, Peter Deming, selected a shorter lens palette than most films I have worked on, so achieving natural roundness was a relatively straightforward process because his subsequent framing choices significantly benefited 3D. I am as much a fan of beautiful bokeh as anyone else, but the process involved to get such bokeh tends to subtract from the ability to get good 3D, and I was happy that when we needed a close-up in this movie, our cameras actually got closer to the subject. Additionally, since many of our shots were over bluescreen, I could take advantage of the coveted "multi-cam" technique. This allowed us to capture individual elements at their own appropriate volumes without the limitations of accommodating the empty Z space between the elements of the foreground and the background.

In each of these films, my goal was to create "good 3D," certainly. However, that definition of what makes "good 3D" is something that changes depending on who you ask, and their individual experience and knowledge of 3D. As stereographers, the best thing we can do is to inform the decision-making members of a production about the cinematographic language of 3D, and then hope we get to practice our art in full cooperation with the other visual storytelling tools of the film. If we play our politics correctly, and communicate the art correctly, we will have carte blanche to use 3D in a way that supports the story. If, for whatever reason, we are unable to communicate that art, we risk having the production's inexperience with (and even fear of) 3D limit our stereo choices; thereby limiting our ability to support the story with 3D.

In the most minimal situation, a stereographer is quietly sitting by a 3D monitor, adapting to the framing, lensing, and composition choices of the production, and adapting the 3D to those decisions, for better or for worse. In the best situation, a stereographer is working together with the director and the cinematographer to create cohesive images that tell the story of each shot on every frame.

DAVE DRZEWIECKI is a cinematographer with over 25 years of extensive experience in every film and video format. He was stereographer on *Pirates of the Caribbean 4, Journey 2: Mysterious Island, Nitro Circus: the Movie 3D, Foo Fighters: Back & Forth, Maroon 5 Concert,* and many other productions, including the live television broadcast in 3D of the 2012 Tournament of Roses Parade.

Drzewiecki writes:
Journey 2: Mysterious Island was conceived and created as a natively photographed 3D movie. Producers Charlotte Huggins and Beau Flynn followed their groundbreaking original *Journey To the Center of the Earth 3D* with this larger and equally successful sequel.

The challenge with any 3D movie is the need to balance the realities of filmmaking schedules and creativity. Even though 3D was a key component to the production, we all knew that it was likely that the majority of viewers would still see it in 2D throughout the initial release in theaters and at home. This meant that rethinking of composition and reconceiving of the narrative patterns just for 3D wasn't going to be applied on this project. The stereoscopic image however, was used very effectively in the visual effects sequences where composition and creative elements could be controlled within the stereo window.

The live action cinematography was shaped in a similar manner to conventional 2D cinematography due to the demanding schedule and large cast. Brad Peyton had the responsibility of delivering each day as planned, which meant the style of the narrative was traditional in the coverage on dialogue and action. Working with slight adjustments to camera angles and compositions were often enough so that the stereo window was respected and the final convergence pass in post could allow some freedom to move the images dimensionally as needed.

As the stereographer, I chose to use a 3 percent maximum background parallax with soft backgrounds and 2 percent with in-focus backgrounds. We would often shoot a second camera. As in traditional coverage, that second camera had a longer focal length lens, which at times would be 85 mm. In that case, our first consideration was to adjust the interaxial (IA) and convergence so that the image would flow and cut with what would likely be the proceeding and following shots. At all times the stereo window was respected and when we could not change the composition to allow for an increased depth flowing into the theater (negative) space, we would have to converge on the closest image touching the lateral edges of the screen.

The film's director, Brad Peyton, was sensitive to coverage such as over-the-shoulder shots and used them as infrequently as possible, but when he felt he needed those shots, he would try to compose them a bit more loosely. Potential window violations were corrected by converging at that point in space and then reducing the IA. When all else failed, floating windows were added in postproduction to change the apparent position of the screen relative to the image.

In all *Journey 2: 3D* is a very pleasant, consistent 3D movie that I think is best viewed on a 3D TV. I feel that way with all 3D images. I think the larger theater screens and its "mellowed" depth and the resultant darker screen brightness takes away from the impact of the smaller, brighter 3D TV fun. See it from a 3D Blu-Ray!

ROB ENGLE began his career in stereoscopic filmmaking in 2004 when he supervised the adaptation of *The Polar Express for IMAX 3D* theaters. In addition to the films described below, his 3D feature credits include *Monster House, Open Season, Cloudy With a Chance of Meatballs, Green Hornet, Pirates of the Caribbean: On Stranger Tides,* and *The Smurfs.* Rob's experience spans the breadth of 3D techniques from conversion to native-3D live-action capture to rendered-CG.

Engle writes:
I've been fortunate to have been involved in numerous stereoscopic features since our work on *The Polar Express: The IMAX 3D Experience* in 2004. These films have used every technique commonly used today including native rendered CG, native stereoscopic photography, and 2D to 3D conversion. For these notes I have chosen three representative films, each using a different technique and representing different phases of the modern 3D era.

In Robert Zemeckis' 2007 performance-capture epic tale *Beowulf*, the hero must fight the monster Grendel, make a deal with Grendel's mother, and eventually battle a giant dragon in the skies over his kingdom. While the film features plenty of action the story centers around the shifting fortunes of the title character.

Beowulf was Sony Pictures Imageworks' second performance-capture film with Zemeckis and it was important to the 3D team going into it that we maximize the benefits of the 3D medium while also ensuring that viewers did not come away with headaches. After doing some initial testing with depth choices for the director it was decided that, in general, we would converge the film such that the subject would play just on the audience side of the screen with a pre-determined maximum positive parallax for background objects. For key action scenes and 3D moments we would naturally increase the 3D effect as needed.

While we had used the multi-camera technique in limited cases on *Open Season,* our software environment for *Beowulf* allowed us full, interactive 3D previewing of multi-camera shots on the big screen. This added flexibility meant that we could use the technique far more often. One of the primary uses of the multi-camera technique was a somewhat experimental modulation of the 3D space to support the emotional state of the characters. As a general rule, when a character was in a position of power (or at least thought he was) we would subtly increase the roundness of the character without changing the overall depth of the shot. For scenes in which a character was in a relative position of weakness we would tend to flatten them out.

Another use of multi-camera technique came out of a side-effect of the subject matter. Since much of the story of *Beowulf* takes place at night with only torches for lighting, many scenes were very contrasty. In those circumstances we would use multi-camera cheats to bring the background closer to the screen in order to reduce ghosting in the BG while ensuring an adequate degree of character roundness.

Beowulf also marked our first use of floating windows. On this film we tended to use them as a purely technical pass to fix edge violations but also found occasional places where a deeper window would enhance the feeling of viewer to subject distance in a point-of-view shot.

With the digital release completed, we proceeded to tune the film for its IMAX 3D film release. This included reconverging the 3D to fit the IMAX parallel exhibition style and enhancing select scenes to make the 3D effect more pronounced/intimate, bringing the characters further into the audience.

In the 2009 Disney film *G-Force* a group of guinea pigs band together with other furry critters to save the world from an unknown force intent on world domination. Shot on film and using substantial computer graphics to realize the main characters, the 3D release utilized a hybrid of 2D to 3D conversion and native-stereo CG rendering to achieve the stereoscopic effect.

With a mandate that the 3D on the film should be memorable (one studio executive quipped that he wanted people to remember the film "was in 3D more than it was about guinea pigs"), director Hoyt Yeatman fully embraced the medium.

For scenes in which the audience was at the level of the guinea pigs the director wanted there to be a strong sense that the audience matched the guinea pigs in size. Inter-axial camera separations would be chosen that closely matched the eye spacing of the subjects and the camera would be kept at their eye level. Variations on these settings were typically employed for effect such as when we wanted to accentuate the proportions of the star-nosed mole, Speckles. Close-ups of the characters often employed soft focus backgrounds allowing us to use multi-camera techniques to emphasize the roundness of characters while diminishing the background details.

For scenes in which the house fly agent, Mooch, was in flight, strong negative parallax was employed to maximize the 3D effect.

Additionally, the climax of the film features a giant robot constructed of thousands of appliances. It was important to the director that we avoid miniaturization, obviating the need for more human-scale camera separation.

In order to enhance and emphasize the off-screen effects in the film, we utilized a release aspect ratio of 1.85:1 which was letter-boxed for 2.35:1 presentation. The result was a black mask on the top and bottom of the frame, which we would occasionally break into with key objects. Of particular note was the pet shop snake attack early in the film. In order to heighten the 3D effect, when the snake lunged at camera, its jaws overlapped the black masking. Later in the film, we would even use the technique for more subtle effects, like having flying debris or key props extend over the mask, enhancing the sense of being in the space of the film.

At one point we even experimented with printing an explicit pattern on the picture mask area to give a much clearer cue as to where the screen played in depth. This idea was quickly dropped after the team realized the pattern would make the whole film feel like a stage play or storybook because you become acutely aware of the frame edges. Nevertheless, it was an interesting experiment and the technique might make sense for a different kind of film.

Finally, given that the visual effects were meant to be believable photo-real representations that needed to blend seamlessly with the photographed plates, it was just as important that the quality of the 3D conversion needed to match that of the native CG stereo renders. As a result we had a very high bar set for the conversion quality, even though this film was the first feature to use these techniques.

While the 2012 release of Columbia Pictures' *The Amazing Spider-Man* revisited the origin of the title character's powers, director Marc Webb also wanted to introduce a new cast, a new villain, and utilize 3D to bring the world of Spider-Man to life in a whole new way. "Realism" was the key aesthetic mission for the film. This would set it apart from past films about the wall-crawler, so much so that a large number of Spider-Man's feats would either directly feature stunt performers or use their actions as a springboard for intricate digital stunt doubles brought to life by Sony Pictures Imageworks. The goal of realism also strongly influenced the decision to capture the majority of the film using native 3D photography.

Given that Spider-Man tends to spend a lot of time swinging from tall buildings it was only natural that, in mid-2010, pre-production testing began on a 30-story high-rise hotel in downtown Los Angeles. That day of testing as well as other subsequent days (which included everything from intimate close-ups of actors to dropping dummies off the side of the hotel) allowed Webb and D. P. John Schwartzman, ASC to come up with a style of 3D which would directly support the way in which Marc wanted to tell the story. The key feature of this style was to modulate the use of depth to match the dramatic content of the story. For mostly narrative and dialog-driven scenes, the 3D effect would be dialed back to ensure the audience was not distracted by it, while for action scenes, the effect would be increased with the occasional overt "3D moment." This explicit modulation of 3D depth had the added advantage that we were using the entire dynamic range of 3D. Bigger moments were more effective since they stood out in relation to the lesser, dramatic 3D. This is very similar to the way in which sound design is done ... allowing the sound to be quiet so as to emphasize the louder moments (one cannot make something feel louder if everything is loud).

Once the photography was completed, visual effects work on the film could begin in earnest. While a significant portion of the visual effects would make use of 3D plate photography, several key sequences involved fully virtual environments, which allowed us the flexibility to film the action without the limits of physical camera rigs. These environments included an underwater sewer, a high school interior hallway, the skyscrapers of Manhattan's 6th Avenue, and the top of the OsCorp tower where the climactic battle between Spider-Man and the Lizard occurs. The action featured in these environments would utilize the more dynamic 3D treatment, but it was important throughout the film that the cinematography for the fully virtual visual effects shots fit in with the surrounding native-3D photography. For the sequences in which we follow Spider-Man as he swings through the city, it was tempting to increase the inter-axial spacing to that significantly larger than human vision would accommodate. In each of these cases we would carefully watch for miniaturization, which can have the opposite effect by making the environment feel small.

As with most modern 3D films, *The Amazing Spider-Man* featured a small percentage of visual effects and production photography that had been completed in 2D. It was important on this production to ensure that the converted photography blend in seamlessly with the native stereo photography and rendered 3D visual effects.

JAMES GOLDMAN is a camera assistant, and stereographer. His 3D credits include *Pirates of the Caribbean: On Stranger Tides, Prometheus,* and *Oz: The Great and Powerful.*

Goldman writes:

The craft of 3D filmmaking has undergone massive changes in the last five years – monitoring technology has improved, the 3D cameras and rigs themselves have become more stable and user-friendly, post-convergence processes have gone from bad to great. No matter what kind of technological advances are made, the physical craft of choosing an IA, where to set convergence, and how a film will cut from shot to shot has basically remained the same and often become more challenging with modern filmmaking. In an industry that now relies heavily on visual effects for certain films, a 3D department's job can at times be more difficult than ever. When you cannot see what will actually be in the frame or what backgrounds will exist in the finished product, one is forced to rely on place markers and reference points to estimate a depth range and push the IA as far as possible without over doing it.

In the last couple of years I have been fortunate enough to work on some amazing projects with some incredible directors and cameramen. I was introduced to 3D on *Alice in Wonderland.* While the movie was shot in 2D and later converted, I had the chance to pick the brains of the visual effects department as to what they were looking for, what helped them in post, and also what hindered the 3D. Shortly after, I found myself on *Pirates of the Caribbean 4,* where I learned stereo applications from Dave Drzewiecki and took over as stereographer for the London portion of the film. While in London I was asked by Dariusz Wolski, the DP of *Pirates,* to do a couple of days of testing for Ridley Scott in 3D for an upcoming film.

After testing was done for *Prometheus* it was decided that the film would be shot in native 3D. *Prometheus* was set up as a massive visual effects show from inception and the studio, along with the visual effects supervisor and myself, all agreed that shooting parallel would be the easiest, most cost-effective way to execute what was planned for the film. Shooting parallel can have two meanings; one is when the farthest object in visible sight is converged upon, making it very close to parallel. The other practice is that the cameras truly live in a parallel state. This means that neither camera is toed in at all. For Pirates 4 we converged on the farthest point; for *Prometheus* the decision was made to shoot true parallel.

The reason for shooting parallel in most cases is cost. Imagine alien landscapes all generated in CG. Now imagine pulling convergence and IA as the hero walks towards the camera in that world. What you have is two cameras that are seeing completely different angles and changing in multiple ways throughout the shot. This causes problems for visual effects when you have to constantly be changing the perspective of the one camera. Problems equal money and the less money that you have to spend on CG elements the more can be spent on the building of sets, or the lighting design, or any number of things that can make a massive difference in the final product. Shooting parallel and only pulling IA is much less bothersome to match in the final CG process of all elements. Shooting parallel also offers more control in the post world when a convergence pass is applied to the entire film in regards to the continuity of the look of the film. People would argue that when shooting parallel, you lose a certain roundness quality that you get when converged. I would agree with this on certain specialty shots and also on close-ups of people's faces or objects.

On *Prometheus*, extensive testing was done on make-up, costumes, and even landscapes. All the testing was shot in 3D and also shot parallel and converged so that the difference could be seen beforehand and decisions could be made as to what shots would be cheated and shot converged for maximum effect. Both Ridley and Dariusz are extremely visual and right away could see the benefits for shooting certain elements of the film converged. A perfect example of that is with the spacesuit shields. When shot converged in the close-ups, there was a noticeable difference in the curvature of the helmets that added depth unlike what was seen in a parallel set-up. For a majority of the close-ups through the helmets we stuck to the converged decision and everyone was happy. We shot a handful of specialty shots throughout the film converged: things jumping out, holograms, and some extreme close-up cutaways. However, for the most part, the film was shot parallel.

Shooting parallel doesn't mean that you do not know what it is going to look like converged. I have multiple 3D monitors at my station as well as at the video village. Ridley watched everything in 3D at his village. At my station, the rig techs and myself would all watch rehearsals converged in as many ways as we had time to so that we could keep ourselves on the same page from shot to shot to maintain a depth limit within each scene. After decisions were made with the IA, notes would be passed to video assist so that Ridley could watch a converged image from every camera live. The system worked well, but Ridley likes to shoot multiple cameras, often four, and many times it was important to ask him where one shot died and the others became relevant. Frequently throughout filming there would be three of us pulling IAs all day long. It kept everyone on his or her toes for sure. I was very fortunate to have two of the best rig techs working today, Steve Evans and Frank Fisher, both of who knew and understood practical 3D.

The lines of communication were open on set and, thanks to an excellently designed system by Ryan Nguyen, our DIT, everyone could stay close enough to one another to maintain a dialog as the shooting was taking place. It didn't take Ridley and Dariusz long to start noticing the foreground issues that 3D can have if you're not careful. Ridley, who loves to dolly from behind things and expose the world of his set and actors, quickly noticed that if he pulled the camera back a little we could create the depth with the 3D unlike 2D practices. It was a pleasure to work with two gentlemen who so embraced the idea of making a 3D film.

It was also very helpful to everyone that we watched dailies everyday in 3D and not 2D, as I have heard some people do. Watching in 3D opens everyone's eyes to what you are actually doing and what can be done. Often we would shoot different variations of certain shots, some with strong foreground, as Ridley liked, some with less, as I liked. Being able to watch the difference on a big screen was incredibly helpful in getting across certain points and showing everyone the differences in the look of the shots I was fighting for. I didn't always win those fights but at least I had the opportunity to try. The whole idea of the 3D for *Prometheus* was to maintain a mild look within the spaceship, giving everything depth and shape but not to ever exaggerate anything. The ship played well in 3D because everything was narrow and long. It was easy to make it look deep and alive when everything had such detail in it. Once they landed on the alien planet, the goal was to open it up and try to make them feel smaller than usual without causing any kind of miniaturizing effect. The opening scene of the engineer near the waterfall was shot using the maximum IA possible. Ridley wanted that world to seem removed and desolate. The move from that world to a small cave in the next sequence I feel highlighted the massiveness of the opening scene.

I'm not sure if that effect has an actual name, but I always refer to it as barreling. For some reason, when you have actors in a room of odd size and shape or in an open landscape and you open up the IA to an extreme, you get a strange illusion that seems to make them look smaller than they would naturally. It has a lot to do with the length of the lens, the angle the camera is shooting them at, and the environment itself. We did testing within the spaceship just to make sure we knew how far we could go without this happening. We actually used the trick intentionally while shooting the reveal of the massive head sculpture in the ampule room. As the camera pulls away and across the back of the head, we stretched the IA out as far as we could go to give the effect of the room being larger than it was. It worked so well it made it in the film.

One of the biggest conditions we used to our advantage while shooting was the lack of light within the alien building. While many critics of 3D have commented that it doesn't work in low light situations, we found that you could use an out-of-focus background that itself was under-lit by multiple stops to push for larger IAs. If the background is dark and out of focus, your eyes naturally pay it less attention and focus more on what is exposed and in focus. The eyes have a tendency to be drawn to the light. While shooting in the caves with all the actors wearing the spacesuits, we would completely forget about the background and focus on just the helmet lights to decide our depth. Using just those lights, we built our foreground, midground, and background elements by the position of actors within the space. The dark walls were just there, almost in the extreme background by the time it was over. To a certain extent, I feel the dark actually helped to create a different kind of 3D look for the interiors of the alien world in comparison to the ship where everything was visible.

Prometheus was such an amazing opportunity and I learned so much of the practical uses of what 3D could accomplish that I was excited to do another film and even try and push it farther. Luckily for me, as I was finishing up, I was contacted by Peter Demming about a film *Oz: The Great and Powerful*. He was looking for a stereographer who had experience in shooting parallel and also in dealing with vast CG elements. I was excited to do another film in 3D, but I was also thrilled to work with another great cameraman, as well as the director, Sam Rami. The DIT from *Prometheus*, Ryan Nguyen, and myself were both hired to do the film.

The set-up of the show was much easier than *Prometheus*; they had a video supervisor, Ian Kelly, who set everything up before we even arrived. Also, because of the massive visual effects involved in the film, they had a stereo supervisor who would be on set and carry the film all the way through post. Ed Marsh was the supervisor and has been around 3D longer than most. It was great to have someone to bounce ideas off of and also hear his thoughts on my work. Ed, along with Ian, set up a great 3D projection screening room for dailies. It was clear from the beginning that the 3D was important to the people making the film.

It was decided long before I was on the show that *Oz* was to be shot parallel, for much the same reason as Prometheus, only the scope of *Oz*, as far as what they were going to do in terms of visual effects, dwarfed *Prometheus*.

Walking into stages where you had no idea what was going to be behind the actors when the film was done was a little intimidating. Luckily, there were excellent pre-visualized animated storyboards that we could watch to see just what the idea was for that environment of the day. The visual effects team was also very helpful whenever there was any question about what was in frame or how close it was going to come to camera; Scott Stockdyke, the visual effects supervisor, had the answers. It was key on *Oz* that the visual effects department consisted of some of the best in the business; they had so much to deal with everyday. From the 3D side, it was very beneficial having the 3D supervisor around. He would give a heads up about what shots were coming that should be bigger and also kept the lines of communication open with all departments.

Oz was such a different movie to work on than Prometheus in terms of lighting and depth. *Oz* was a big, bright, open realm. Rami and Demming constructed a world that they wanted everyone to see. *Oz* was meant to be enjoyed and they wanted the audience to be sucked into it. Working the 3D in this environment was challenging. It was a different kind of depth, a depth where you could see the actors coming from a stage-length away. There was a lot of opportunity to watch them grow through the frame and into the foreground. The opportunity to go big with the 3D was there at every turn. The idea for me was to find a larger constant depth level than other films had in the past, to try and really make *Oz* a different looking place.

The visual effects team and I viewed most of the 3D on set. Rami is a very focused director. He meticulously works out each shot, first the move of the camera and the incorporation of all the background actors and then with his main actors. He cares about every detail, but he focuses himself on the important things that directors should do with their actors. He knew every shot that was important to him and when he wanted the 3D to be big. The rest of the time most of my feedback came from his long-time editor, Bob Murawski. Bob watches dailies religiously, sometimes twice a day. He was always pushing the 3D. He would say, "We're making a 3D movie, aren't we?"

One of the more difficult things to deal with in the film was the amount of light. While it is very helpful in seeing everything and creating depth, it can also work against the 3D. When you have massive spaces and everything is visible, often times the separation depth becomes that much stronger. For example, a medium close-up with a large IA leaves no room to converge but on the actor. Sometimes that convergence on the actor can make the world behind them seem to go on forever, in an unnatural looking way. Everything really boils down to preference; you like it and you think it looks good, or you don't. No two people have the same 3D experience from the same film because everyone's eyes and brains process images differently. The goal is to try and make the image comfortable and at the same time vibrant for everyone.

One of the ways we sometimes tried to make the 3D bigger and at the same time enjoyable was to slow it down. When the brain has more time to process the image, it makes it seem bigger and easier to cut to and away from. Things coming towards the camera are easier to see in any format when they are slowed down. It gives the viewers' brain that little extra bit of time to realize what it is. We would often shoot multiple frame rates so that later it could be decided which worked the best.

3D is not a medium for everyone, viewer and filmmaker alike. There are always going to be shots that just do not work as well as others. Over the shoulder conversation shots never work well, but that is what narrative filmmaking is all about. At that moment, 3D takes the back seat and you just dial in the IA as well as you can without compromising the shot. 3D is only one tool in telling a great story. Films are made every day and have been for years without 3D. It would be ridiculous to think that a certain set of rules should be applied to a film shooting in 3D that are not to 2D. Being able to have a dialog with the director and cinematographer as to what may work better in certain situations is key. It's difficult to tell people who have been making films for years that you can't do something or that it doesn't work. That kind of conversation I have seen backfire on people, including myself. It has to be an adaptable medium that works with filmmakers and not against them. Also, certain types of films lend themselves better to 3D than others. Action and fantasy films seem better suited to the medium than a romantic comedy. The elements involved and the way they are executed make all the difference in the world to obtaining a better image. 3D will come and go as it has for the last 50 years. Hopefully, each time it comes back, the technology will be better at the production end as well as the display end, making it increasingly more enjoyable for all.

ED W. MARSH is a New York Times best-selling writer and filmmaker living in Los Angeles. His work in 3D includes the James Cameron documentary projects *Ghosts of the Abyss* and *Aliens of the Deep*, as well as *Journey to the Center of the Earth*, *The Chronicles of Narnia: Voyage of the Dawn Treader*, *Green Lantern*, and *Harry Potter and the Deathly Hallows, Part Two*. He is currently the Stereoscopic Supervisor on Disney's *Oz: The Great and Powerful*. Marsh also enjoys working in both 2D and 1D, more commonly referred to as radio.

Marsh writes:
"It was a picture of a ship – a ship sailing straight towards you."
The Chronicles of Narnia: The Voyage of the Dawn Treader

I have a love/hate relationship with stereo filmmaking. I personally enjoy the effect, but I don't think it is necessary for every film. I will seek out 3D screenings but I too dislike having to pay extra for the tickets. If the introduction of sound didn't cause a rise in ticket prices then why should 3D? Then there is the matter of technical compromise. Yes, you have less light. Yes, action can strobe more than in 2D. (I'm convinced these limitations will get better or disappear.) Lastly, you have to deal with the fact that a stereo aesthetic has been slow to emerge. Producers shouting that they want the 3D "in their lap" or "hitting the back of the theater" should question their grasp on basic anatomy and physics, because my eyes are in my head, not my lap, thank you very much, and I have never been able to see what is behind me, either. I've often wondered if the introduction of color caused a similar fracas in

Hollywood. Were there producers screaming for the magenta of their starlet's dress to bleed? Were there pre-internet trolls gathering in basements and grousing about how the color yellow was totally missing from some scenes?

All that said, I felt very lucky to be asked to supervise the stereo conversion of *The Chronicles of Narnia: The Voyage of the Dawn Treader* for Twentieth Century Fox. The book had been a personal favorite as a child, rich with characters I had wanted to meet and places I had wanted to visit. I also felt very nervous: Fox had decided to convert the film after shooting had all but been completed; VFX were well underway; the director, Michael Apted, was skeptical; and *Clash of the Titans* had just been released, raising the question throughout the industry as to whether or not you could successfully convert a full-length motion picture without killing the patient on the table (box office profits aside). All due respect to the artists on *Clash*; they did pioneering work under very limited circumstances. They simply needed much more time.

We *had* time. I was brought on in April to break down the edit and develop a plan of attack. I worked with both the director and the editor Rick Shaine, who were extremely giving of their time and curious about how stereo might affect their choices. I proposed modest changes and in some cases they agreed to accommodate. I worked with the VFX artists, gently suggesting that the shot of the mouse with the sword might play better in stereo if the sword's tip were angled *just so,* allowing us to register depth all along the length of the blade. My goal was to harvest and take advantage of the many stereo opportunities the film afforded me without compromising the 2D version of the film and without getting in the way of the story.

And this is where *Dawn Treader* had one distinct advantage. 3D is actually built into the story in some very fun ways. There are invisible characters who are first glimpsed as eerie disturbances, kind of like heat ripples. On James Cameron's *Ghosts of the Abyss* we had several underwater shots, which had a flare in one eye but not in the other. We cleaned these up by taking the flare-free eye and cloning the pixels into the flared image. It required much more work to make it look good and some of the early experiments left you with mind-bending "holes" in reality that were very intriguing to the eye. It really felt like a three-dimensional version of what a cloaking device might look like. A milder variation of this technique informed the stereo work on the many invisible Dufflepud creatures.

However, the most story-specific 3D moment happens when Lucy, Edmund, and Eustace travel to Narnia. They are studying a painting of a Narnian-looking ship when that ship starts to move. "In front of him was not glass but real sea, and wind and waves," writes Lewis. Quickly, the ocean pushes through the frame and into the room and soon after that they are engulfed by the shockingly blue water of the Narnian Sea. The painting has become a window, a portal to another world.

The scene is a stereo filmmaker's dream! Taking a flat painting and pulling it into dimensionality. Establishing a sky and horizon beyond the dimensions of the cramped bedroom. And transitioning from that rather plain environment into the full volumetric fun of being underwater, where every little bubble and piece of particulate helps define space in pleasing ways. VFX Supervisor Angus Bickerton was well along with the painting's animation before I came on board. I was lucky he'd chosen to work in a full 3D CGI environment (and then render it with a painterly look reminiscent of artist Joseph Turner). This made it a relatively simple affair to define the other eye and then open up from a monocular view of the painting to a stereo view. We found that this effect was modestly hindered by the painting treatment so we found a way to transition to more realistic textures sooner. The original shot was also meant to be a bit shorter, but when Apted saw the effect in stereo he was convinced to lengthen it as much as reasonable without causing a strange pause in the action for 2D audiences. This was also true for the shots of the painting in which the sky and ocean stretch out beyond the dimensions of the room. In the shot where Eustace takes the painting off the wall, the editor had cut away because it didn't feel right in 2D. "I thought it looked like a mistake," Apted later told me. In 3D the shot suddenly took on new meaning since the painting was now a window and the space beyond the wall held our interest. In the 3D release of the film this shot is longer than in the 2D release for this reason. (Not by much. There was no separate mix for the 3D release of the film; we shortened the incoming shot to maintain sync). And then in the shot when the water finally fills the room and we transition from surface to underwater, we took advantage of the natural magnification that happens when cameras go underwater by ramping up the depth of our conversion by a hyperbolic but still comfortable amount.

Of course, we settled down and brought depth to the rest of the film as well, but never did the stereo take as much of the limelight as it did for that one story-specific sequence. And I'm happy to report that the director was pleased enough with the end result that he thanked me as his "stereo guru" in front of the Queen of the United Kingdom at the film's Royal Premier that December. That's not really a job title you can put on your resume but I was very proud and grateful for the gesture.

People often complain that 3D is merely a gimmick that the studios have latched onto in order to grab a greater profit. And, sometimes, I would have to agree. But I also know that when it is done with care and in concert with talented visual storytellers, 3D can take you places you've always wanted to go.

The painting has become a window, a portal to another world.

SEAN PHILLIPS is one of the most experienced 3D directors/cinematographers in the world. He was director of photography and stereographer on the groundbreaking giant screen films *Wild Safari 3D* and *Encounter in the Third Dimension in IMAX 3D*. He has shot 3D films for documentaries, visual effects, a variety of theme parks, and was the stereographer on Peter Jackson's King Kong 360 3D attraction at Universal Studios.

Phillips writes:
The best way to begin the stereo design of a film is to do a series of screenings and tests and look at them on a screen as big as what you'd see in a larger theater in which audiences are likely to view the film. This is because a larger theater will represent the wider extremes of viewing conditions that an audience is likely to encounter watching your film. When you move around a large 3D screening room you will begin to notice that a stereo space may look normal in the center seats but appear compressed in the front row seats and expanded in the back row seats. (If you are doing a special venue film that only plays in one theater, it's essential to use only that theater or replicate its dimensions for all screenings.) Watch tests and dailies from the front and back as well as the center and side seats. Bring in test viewers, especially those from the age group most likely to see the film. Young people will accept

far more adventurous 3D than older audiences. These types of tests and screenings are done too rarely but the results are always amazing, especially for first-time filmmakers. Even for experienced 3D filmmakers these screenings are important because perceptual recollections fade over time and stereographers need reminding as much as anyone exploring the medium.

I remember working with a director who hadn't done a 3D film before but was eager to learn and experiment. He wanted to push what had been done and try things out involving close foreground objects. The schedule was tight but we made the time to shoot a day of tests and then view them on a full-sized screen. While shooting the tests I'd mention what I thought would and wouldn't work, and when I thought what we were shooting would be safe and when it was likely to be difficult to view. In the course of the screening he agreed with most of my predictions and that his original ideas wouldn't work, at least in camera. As the stereographer I had earned his confidence in much the same way that a director does with his D.P. In the course of the next few days we reconceived the stereo design of the film and shot foreground objects against green screen in order to create the foreground effect in 3D that was watchable and pleasing for an audience. He scaled back some of his ideas, but in the end he was able to achieve his vision, something that would have been impossible without testing.

In one film I did, the last 3D scene involved an older man giving a new watch to a young boy. The film was book-ended in a 2D present day and what happened in between took place in the future in 3D. The 3D was very immersive in its design, meaning that much of the action was played off-screen in theater space (personal space), also called negative parallax. The new watch was very significant in the story and the director wanted to bring the watch very far out into theater space to emphasize the importance of the gift.

The challenge of the scene was to go from a two-shot to a much tighter shot of the older actor's hand extending the watch far into theater space, then a reverse angle of the boy's hand taking the watch, and back to the two-shot. The first two-shot was done with the actors at about a 1 percent negative offset. During this first two-shot the older actor began to extend his hand toward the boy. Over the cut he continues extending his hand, now more directly to camera and in a much tighter framing, revealing that he's holding a futuristic watch. At the beginning of this closer shot, the hand started at about a 1.5 percent negative offset, extending out to a maximum of 5 percent. Because the hand extended from a lesser offset to a larger one, it allows audiences to accept that an off-screen object can appear quite close to their faces, in a way that could never be done in a direct cut. In the next shot, a reverse angle, the boy pulled the watch back from camera, bridging the strong negative offset between the cut and drawing the viewers' eyes back toward the screen plane to a 1.5 percent negative offset, at which point we cut back to the two-shot with the actors back at a 1 percent negative offset. When viewed in motion, the shots cut naturally and not only gave us some very immersive 3D but also a very consistent sense of movie space.

There seems to be an army of novice stereographers who think that shooting 3D is just a matter of adjusting convergence and interaxial so that it fits a stereo bracket around a convergence point on a monitor that overlays the left and right eyes. If a monitor is used, it is critical to make sure the left and right eye images are reconciled so that they are identically scaled and devoid of geometric errors and vertical or horizontal misalignments. If not, the live stereo overlay will give false values, which usually result in reduced interaxials that flatten the depth of the shot. This technique is often necessary in live-switch multi-camera or documentary shooting conditions, but should rarely be used in rehearsed scenes.

In a rehearsed scene actors have marks, the camera has a clearly designed path, and focus pullers carefully anticipate and adjust for the actor's actual positions. This should also be true of the stereo adjustments. During the shot the stereographer (and/or his deputy) is making these adjustments of IA and convergence in much the same way as the focus puller pulls focus, and like a focus puller not just to the actor's marks but also to compensate for deviations in the actors and the camera's positions for any given point in time. Trying to do this visually off an overlay monitor usually results in delays and errors in the stereo adjustments during the take. To avoid this, the best way is to set marks on the handset just like the focus pullers do. You can use the monitor to determine the marks, but ideally a good 3D rig should be able to give the stereographer accurate readouts right on the handset. For the IA, these should be in inches or millimeters. Never use centimeters for IA as they can be confused with inches in shooting and post environments that often mix metric and imperial values, like here in the USA. No one wants to be wondering in post VFX if it's 2.5 centimeters or 2.5 inches on an IA setting. In contrast, no one is going to confuse 63 millimeters or 25 millimeters with inches.

The convergence setting should be in feet and inches or decimal meters, just like focus. With this information you can pull convergence and IA even without a monitor, and this is something a stereographer should be able to do if an overlay monitor fails, or if one is not available when needed. There are a number of respectable apps that stereographers can use to confirm that marks are good, and many stereographers have written their own apps or Excel templates to give them reliable stereo information without using overlay monitors. This is not to say that overlay monitors, stereo displays, SIP boxes, and the like aren't great tools and confidence checkers on the set. A veteran stereographer should always be the master of the numbers behind focal lengths, distances, IA, and convergence.

Although there can be profound exceptions, my two central guidelines for shooting in 3D are to keep the camera wider and closer to the subject whenever possible, and to always try to shoot for space. By "shooting for space" I mean that shots are framed so that close subjects are free to play close to the viewer in theater space and far subjects play further away from the viewer either in theater space or behind the screen. This creates a natural and consistent sense of stereo space and scale in the same way that the traditional cutting of close, medium, over-the-shoulders, and reverses facilitates storytelling with actors.

This may sound ridiculously obvious and simple until you actually try to do it, because you will not succeed until you change your basic sense of framing. 2D filmmaking is abstract in the sense that space is represented graphically. In 2D things very close to camera that aren't the subject of the shot are shapes and blurs, graphic but not real objects. In 2D all the real space is at the screen plane and depth cues are *represented*, not *presented* as they are in stereoscopic space. Stereoscopic space demands we respect the nearness of objects because that has helped us to survive for millions of years by avoiding predators and, in my experience, avoiding collisions with objects when fleeing predators, or when hunting prey.

2D framing doesn't need to respect stereo space, but 3D framing has to unless most of the depth is removed from a shot. There are times when this is an acceptable strategy, but if the goal is to use 3D to immerse the audience, your framing has to respect frame breaks on the left and right and avoid competing foreground objects. Floating windows can help offset some of these issues but they have limitations, problems in distribution, and can also be a distraction.

I have been lucky in that I am usually the director of photography as well as the stereographer on projects that I shoot. In the future that will be commonplace. Today, however, a stereographer who is not also the D.P. will find it very difficult to convince a seasoned 2D D.P. to change the way they frame their shots for a 3D film. It is even harder when neither the director nor the D.P. have shot 3D before. Designing and screening tests for D.P.s and directors helps immensely. In time, as more directors and D.P.s work in 3D that will, of course, change, but it has been a tough road and there is, at present, a huge gap between the aesthetic quality that some 3D animated features have achieved and what we've seen in live action features.

Ultimately, the role of the stereographer will merge with that of the D.P. It is only a matter of time. The grammar of 3D storytelling is still evolving, but that's what makes it so worth being a part of. Technology is also advancing in ways that will ease this transition. Today's mirror rigs look, admittedly, like science projects. Within five years, however, camera systems and imaging software will have evolved to the point where shooting in full 3D will be little more complicated than 2D shooting is today.

DEMETRI PORTELLI has been working as a professional cameraman for 17 years. He trained in 3D on *Resident Evil*. He was the stereographer on *Hugo, 47 Ronin,* and *The Selected Works of T. S. Spivet.*

Portelli writes:

On *Hugo*, we went to London with a mirror rig and two prototype Alexa cameras to shoot the first digital film for Mr. Scorsese and his first foray into 3D filmmaking. With his vast appreciation for cinematic 3D history Mr. Scorsese was willing to commit himself to shoot the entire film using 3D rigs for the absolute best stereo image capture.

My assignment for every shot was: to manage the distribution of the stereo correctly throughout every frame of the live captured material on every 3D rig; to build the on-screen depth and to find the correct stereo volume for each shot, while pulling IA and/or convergence simultaneously or independently based on the needs of each particular set-up.

It is a collaborative creative journey of exploration and investigation to find the appropriate 3D path for the film. Mr. Scorsese had annotated his script with pencil notes to indicate which 3D moments he had selected and some scenes had pre-visualization animations by Rob Legato's team to assist in our planning process. Mr. Scorsese's advice to me was to pay particular attention to the book by Brian Selznick as the first visual reference.

Instead of imposing 3D "rules" on the filmmaker, it was my mandate to make every shot possible. There were challenges and some tricky moments, but overall this is the correct attitude when bringing your 3D tools to a feature film project.

Examples of tricky 3D shots in *Hugo* were the many shots where Hugo was looking through a very close foreground object. A boy secretly fixes clocks and lives in the walls of the old train station. He looks through these clocks to witness the activities and events around him but all is seen from within the walls and the small corridors of the train station. Hugo watches events from behind an old metal grate. In fact, he eventually climbs out of this grate and dangerously ventures into the train station. When shooting, the metal grate was between 18 to 24 inches from the film plane, giving just enough space for soft lighting between the object and the mirror box (matte box). The same situation occurred early on in shooting with the boy's POV through the large clock face far above the toyshop. At approximately 24 inches from the matte box, a small IA and a close convergence on the grate meant the perspective of the shot fell deep. The angle, the height, and the distance to the actors below in the toyshop placed us, the viewer, into the same physical space as the character that is watching. The 3D has defined physical structures and relationships, which does not happen in 2D. The restrictive walls of the train station or the clock are key elements, which tell the audience exactly where they are. They are outsiders like the orphan boy Hugo. They are with Hugo in his claustrophobic situation and empathy can be felt and understood.

As a tool, 3D gives the audience an active role in the story. The 3D defines the relationship of the audience to the material. The journey of this film is designed to eventually become a very immersive experience and a movement through space.

The experience begins with the character's point of view and the audience's point of view only looking at a world to which neither belong. By the end of the film, the audience is a character too, invited in and moving within the 3D space to observe familiar characters directly before us. The audience is a guest at the final party scene, no longer an outsider, much like Hugo with his new family. It is a celebration of inclusiveness at the end as we move through the hallway in the long-take steadicam shot and join into the parlor and the party.

Thanks to the 3D immersive experience, the audience is not passive. The storytelling device in 3D films is often that "the audience" has an active position or a perspective (possibly as an unknowing participant) in the storytelling experience. This might be comparable to a visit to the theater where actors and actresses perform very close to the audience and sometimes around and throughout the theater space. The eyes of the 3D rig are the eyes of the character or the eyes of the audience. The viewer is given an opportunity "to see" a new experience guided by the manipulations of a filmmaker working in stereo.

Hugo was shot completely converged, to illustrate immediately onset the results and opportunities for the filmmaker. We also wanted the natural capture that only shooting native 3D can provide in replicating human features and human recognition of objects with volume. As stereographer, I was responsible for offering alternate IA variations requested by Mr. Scorsese. Marty would ask "More IA, Demetri?". And in a jesting mood he would often say, "Demetri, don't skimp on the paté." Marty would be aware that more IA was needed if he felt the scene was losing impact. Marty would also remind me, "Demetri, when I am directing the actors it is your responsibility not to miss an opportunity."

Marty was very aware of the proximity relationships that the 3D tools could offer. In the final scene where George Melies decides to take Hugo as his son, Marty told me Ben Kingsley would be crying. He asked that I use the convergence to bring him forward during the dramatic moments in his speech. At that time I explained my position to absolutely capture the full stereo depth on each character within the space, but I felt Marty would also benefit by making much of this subtle adjustment after the edit. With coverage on multiple actors in a large space, the movement of the screen plane depth should be timed later when Marty edits the singles and medium shots on George Melies. In this way, stereo depth control is consistent to capture the volume of each character in the scene, but it should be understood that, like a musical score, we were awaiting a fine-tuning at the 3D mix during the DI (digital intermediate) to finesse these dramatic moments. If the editor decides to hold longer on an important shot, then we have the control in postproduction to alter the relationship of the shots for the audience and bring the character closer or let him drift away. On the flipside, if a shot was cut very short and placed into an action sequence it could be adjusted to flow better with less jumpy depth variations.

All 3D moments can be realized and explored on set immediately to suit the decisions of the filmmaker. For this reason, I used a wireless control so I could check in at the director's 3D monitor, sometimes sitting with Mr. Scorsese, to show variations in IA and convergence. For the big 3D moments, we would "bake-in" very big negative parallax, such as the Station Inspector's dog. Just how far into the audience should the dog's nose protrude for effect? It is important that during the process, the filmmaker can explore his options, therefore designing his style and committing to some moments that would otherwise be unseen opportunities.

This was our approach for the big single of Sasha Baron Cohen leaning toward the children in a menacing moment. We had done several conventional over-the-shoulder shots to cover the scene when Marty asked me how I could get the Station Inspector to come out of the screen. With wide lenses and several over-the-shoulder shots I explained that I would need a "clean single" from Hugo's point of view and we should consider choosing a tighter lens, such as a 32 mm prime. This would allow us to capture the full face of the Inspector without edge violations. Marty encouraged Sasha to lean into the lens gradually with each punctuation, and was immediately delighted with the results. After the first take I was able to push up the IA very high and to completely maximize the 3D effect right up to the threshold of discomfort at the final seconds of the shot. The full IA and convergence placements were decided upon right then, very quickly and organically.

3D films are most often about an experience similar to looking through a window. Mr. Scorsese said in the final weeks of postproduction: "I do not want to look into a window, I want to be sitting on the window edge inside the scene. When the children (the actors) came to set in the morning, I could give them a hug before we started the shoot day. When I see this film now I would like to feel that I can still hug these characters."

If, in a scene, the pieces of a clock are beside you and you feel you are between the clock and the wall with the character, then you, the audience, are joining in the action differently.

It is in a director's overall plan that the 3D storytelling must be allowed to unfold. It is crucial for the filmmaker to develop his own stereo language and vision when crafting his film. A great director hires talented people to offer solutions and possibilities and so the 3D benefits from the collaborative experience of great cinematography, camera operating, composition, art direction, acting, and editing (to name a few).

Live capture technologies combined with the understanding of how to operate the new tools for seamless 3D filmmaking have now advanced to the point that serious artists are shooting in 3D.

APPENDIX B
SUBJECT PLACEMENT AND DEPTH BRACKET

The numbers in the following charts are offered as a general guide to placing the subject of the shot in depth.

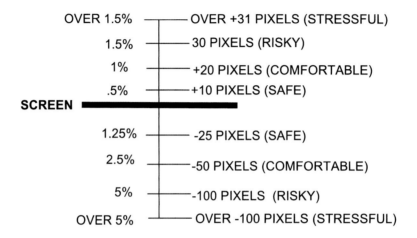

SUBJECT PARALLAX
2K theatre projection on 40-foot

This chart does not refer to the Depth Bracket. The pixel numbers refer to the subject's parallax and its position within the Depth Bracket.

This diagram indicates the values for the subject's parallax on a 40-foot theatre screen. There is a wider range of comfortable viewing in front of the screen than behind it. In front of the screen, a subject's negative parallax up to -25 pixels will be safe and easy to watch; up to a -50 pixel parallax will be comfortable for most viewers; a subject parallax up to -100 pixels will become increasingly more difficult to watch and over -100 pixels will be visually stressful and should be used only for quick visual punctuations.

Behind the screen, in positive parallax, the subject parallax range is smaller. Subject parallax of +10 pixels is very safe and up to +20 pixels is very comfortable for most viewers; subject parallax between +21 to +30 pixels affects visual comfort and a pixel parallax greater than +30 creates hyper-divergence causing eyestrain.

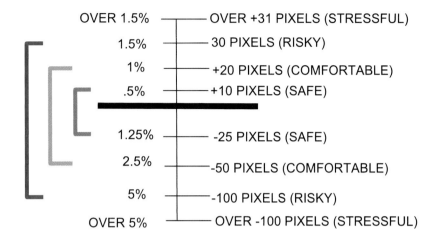

DEPTH BRACKET SIZE
2K theatre projection on 40-foot screen

This diagram can be used as a general rule for the size of the Depth Bracket. Obviously, as the size of the Depth Bracket increases, the amount of depth in the scene increases. The three Depth Bracket examples in the diagram are general examples. The Depth Bracket most appropriate for your production depends on your story and visual style. All of the Depth Bracket examples are taken from successful, modern, digital 3D productions.

A Depth Bracket of about 35 pixels or approximately 1.75 percent (from +10 to –25 indicated with the green bracket) will always create safe, universally acceptable 3D. A Depth Bracket of 70 pixels or about 3.5 percent (from +20 to –50 shown with an orange bracket) will be visually comfortable for most viewers. The largest Depth Bracket is 130 pixels or about 6.5 percent (+30 to -100 in red), which will give the audience the greatest depth range but also create dangerous visual fatigue.

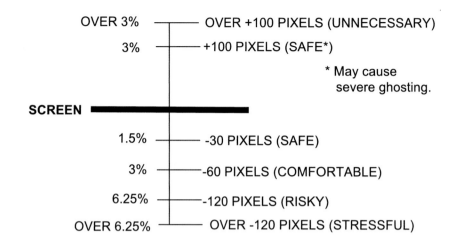

SUBJECT PARALLAX
2K television on 60-inch (diagonally measured)

This chart is a guide for subject placement. These measurements assume a HD 2K television that is 60 inches (measured diagonally) with actual screen dimensions of 52 inches wide and 29 inches high.

When considering the Depth Bracket size for TV and what is stressful or safe, remember that different broadcasters may dictate the allowable 3D limits regardless of what is artistically acceptable. Television parallax limits set by the broadcaster are often conservative because there's a fear of creating visual fatigue, which drives away viewers and reduces advertising revenue. Filmmakers may have to alter their 3D settings to accommodate a variety of broadcast standards.

Depth Bracket Size and Subject vs. Non-Subject

Backgrounds or secondary objects are less sensitive to large parallax settings because, by design, the audience won't look at them with the same attention they give to the subject. Distant mountains, the sky, or peripheral foreground objects won't cause eyestrain because the audience is watching the subject instead.

Time is a critical factor in gauging any 3D visual fatigue. A risky or stressful parallax setting will get worse the longer it stays on the screen. Again, if peripheral objects have a stressful parallax setting they can probably remain on screen longer because the audience isn't looking directly at them.

In 2D and 3D productions, objects that are people, brighter in tone, in-focus, contrasty, moving, or have specific sounds are more likely to attract the audience's point-of-attention. The audience will tend to ignore objects that are unfamiliar, dark, blurry, lack contrast, stationary, or silent. A Depth Bracket can get surprisingly large and push unimportant objects into the extreme foreground and background without creating visual problems. The audience's point-of-attention should remain on the subjects within the visually comfortable area of the Depth Bracket. The more extreme parallax of peripheral non-subjects will usually be ignored so an oversized Depth Bracket won't be a problem. However, peripheral objects with over-exaggerated parallax settings may be so odd-looking that they steal the audience's attention from the subject. Experience and tests are the best way to see how the Depth Bracket can be extended without causing eyestrain.

APPENDIX C
SCREEN RESOLUTION AND DIVERGENCE

Screen Resolution and Divergence

When using pixels to measure parallax you must know the screen size and resolution.

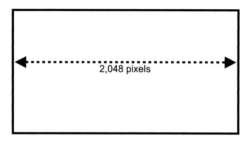

A 2K digital projector in movie theatres has the ability to project an image that is 2,048 pixels wide and 1,080 pixels high, or an aspect ratio of 1.89. But no digital cinema distributor provides a movie in that aspect ratio. The two commercial aspect ratios in use today are 1.85 and 2.40.

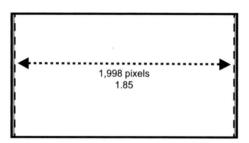

The 1.85 aspect ratio uses a 1998 x 1080 area of the projector's chip (with a tiny amount of Pillar Box vertical borders).

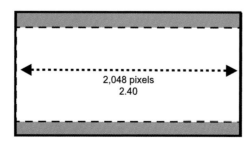

The 2.40 aspect ratio uses a 2,048 x 858 area of the chip (with Letter Box horizontal borders).

In either aspect ratio, a 40-foot screen showing a 2K image has about 4 pixels per horizontal inch. Here's the calculations:

1.85:   40 feet = 480 inches; 1,998 pixels ÷ 480 = 4.16 pixels per inch.
2.40:   40 feet = 480 inches; 2,048 pixels ÷ 480 = 4.26 pixels per inch.

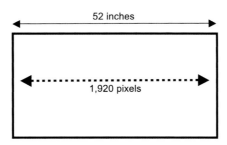

A 60-inch (measured diagonally) HD 2K consumer television has an actual measured screen width of about 52 inches. It, like all consumer 2K televisions, has a horizontal resolution of 1,920 pixels. There are 37 pixels per inch of screen width.

The calculation: 1,920 pixels ÷ 52 inches = 37 pixels per inch.

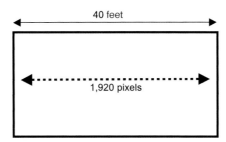

A 40-foot screen with a 1,920 x 1,080 image would have exactly 4 pixels per horizontal inch.

The calculation: 40 feet = 480 inches; 1,920 pixels ÷ 480 = 4 pixels per inch.

For ease of comparison, this book uses 4 pixels per inch for all theatrical motion picture projection and 37 pixels per inch for television screen presentation.

Percentage of screen width or pixels can be used to measure parallax.

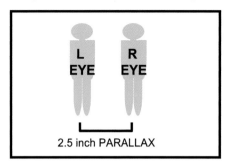

2.5 inch PARALLAX

If the screen measured parallax of an image pair is 2.5 inches or less, there won't be any divergence on any size screen. On a 40-foot motion picture theatre screen 2.5 inches is about 10 pixels or 0.5 percent of the screen width. On a 60-inch (measured diagonally) HD 2K television screen, 2.5 inches is 92 pixels or about 4.75 percent of the screen width.

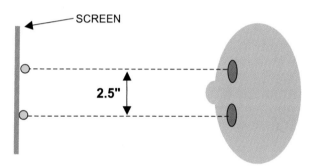

Human eyes are about 2.5 inches apart. When the audience views an image pair with a screen measured parallax of 2.5 inches, their eyes' lines-of-sight will remain parallel.

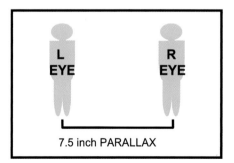

7.5 inch PARALLAX

Divergence occurs when the screen measured parallax exceeds 2.5 inches.

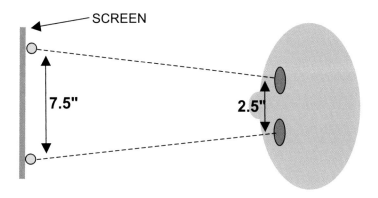

This screen measured parallax is 7.5 inches. The viewer's lines-of-sight diverge to look at the image pair on the screen. Divergence never occurs in real life and eventually causes eyestrain. The combination of the screen measured parallax and the viewer's distance from the screen creates a diverging angle of view for each eye.

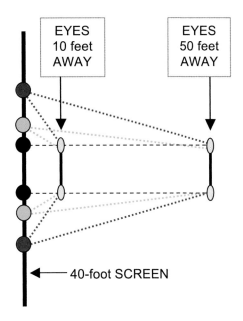

This diagram (not to scale) illustrates how the divergence angle is greater for viewers sitting close to the screen and less for viewers sitting farther away. The closer a viewer sits to the screen the faster divergence eyestrain occurs.

On the diagram, the black circles along the screen represent an image pair 2.5 inches apart. The green circles are an image pair 7.5 inches apart and the red circles are an image pair 10 inches apart. The sight lines for the closer viewer are steeper than the viewer sitting farther away.

	2.5 inch parallax (BLACK)	7.5 inch parallax (GREEN)	10 inch parallax (RED)
10 ft VIEWING DISTANCE	0.0° divergence per eye	1.2° divergence per eye	1.8° divergence per eye
50 ft VIEWING DISTANCE	0.0° divergence per eye	0.25° divergence per eye	0.33° divergence per eye

This table shows the angle of each eye's divergence for viewers sitting 10 feet and 50 feet from the screen.

If the measured screen parallax is 2.5 inches or less, divergence will never occur. Most people can diverge about 0.33 degree to 0.5 degree per eye without causing eyestrain or headaches.

The viewer sitting 10 feet from the screen will have some problems due to divergence. If the measured screen parallax is 7.5 inches, each eye diverges outward approximately 1.2 degrees, which causes eyestrain. A 10 inch measured screen parallax forces each eye to diverge almost 1.5 degrees, which is definitely uncomfortable.

But the viewer sitting 50 feet from the screen and looking at the same parallax will have a very comfortable experience. The 7.5 inch parallax only diverges each eye by 0.25 degree and the 10 inch parallax only causes a 0.33 degree divergence in each eye.

The same situation occurs when watching 3D television. The closer the viewer sits to the TV screen, the more divergence will occur.

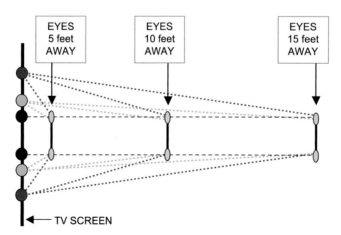

This diagram (above) and table (below) shows the angle of eye divergence for viewers sitting at three different distances from a television.

Creating uncomfortable divergence on a television set requires image parallax that is unnecessarily large and extremely unlikely to ever occur.

	2.5 inch parallax (BLACK)	5 inch parallax (GREEN)	7.5 inch parallax (RED)
5 ft VIEWING DISTANCE	0.0° divergence per eye	1.2° divergence per eye	2.33° divergence per eye
10 ft VIEWING DISTANCE	0.0° divergence per eye	0.66° divergence per eye	1.2° divergence per eye
15 ft VIEWING DISTANCE	0.0° divergence per eye	0.4° divergence per eye	0.8° divergence per eye

This chart indicates the divergent viewing angles but parallax greater than 2.5 inches is rare.

APPENDIX D
STEREOSCOPIC IMAGE PAIRS

Viewer's Left and Right Eye Orientation to a Stereoscopic Image Pair

The position of an object in front of or behind the screen is determined by how the viewer's eyes see the image pair.

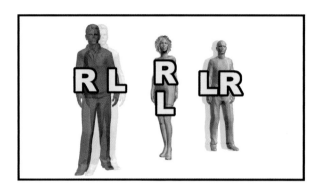

Your eyes receive an object's image pair differently depending on where the object should appear in depth.

Objects appearing on the screen plane (green actor) don't seem to have an image pair but they do. The pair of images is superimposed over each other. Objects that appear on the screen plane have zero parallax separation (***zero parallax setting*** or ***ZPS***).

When an object appears behind the screen plane (blue actor) the image pair is correctly oriented to your eyes. Your left eye looks to the left image and your right eye looks to the right image. Objects that appear behind the screen plane have ***positive parallax***.

When an object appears in front of the screen plane (red actor) the image pair is flipped. The left eye image is offset to the right and the right eye image is offset to the left. Objects that appear in front of the screen plane have ***negative parallax***.

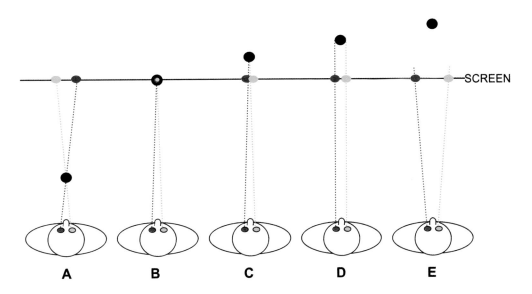

A. Objects appearing in front of the screen require the viewer's eyes to **converge** and **cross**. We converge and cross our eyes when we look at close objects in real life, too. You are converging when you read this book. The difference is that in a 3D movie you are converging in front of the screen even though the image of the object is on the screen surface. Notice that the image pair is flipped. The viewer's left eye sees the screen right image and the viewer's right eye sees the screen left image.

B. Objects that appear on the screen plane require the viewer to **converge** or **cross** at a point on the screen surface.

C. Objects that appear behind the screen require the viewer to **converge** at a point beyond the screen. The image pair is no longer flipped. Now, the viewer's right eye sees the right image and the viewer's left eye sees the left image.

D. Objects appearing at infinity require the viewer's gaze to remain **parallel**. This is similar to what the eyes do in real life when we look at distant objects.

E. Objects with a parallax separation greater than 2.5 inches of measured screen distance will appear farther away than infinity. This causes the eyes to **diverge**.

APPENDIX E
HOW WE SEE 3D

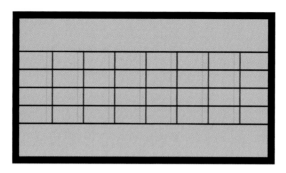

Put on your 3D glasses and look at this grid. The grid appears behind the window. But only the vertical lines in this grid are providing that depth information to your eyes.

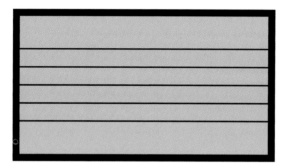

Here is the grid with the vertical lines removed. With or without your 3D glasses, there isn't any depth because horizontals are of no use to your vision system in providing depth information.

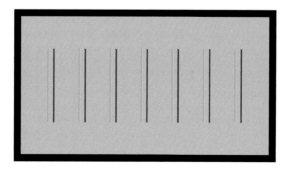

Viewing the verticals only with your 3D glasses instantly creates depth. Our vision system only perceives stereoscopic pairs on the vertical axis as a cue to depth because our eyes are side by side.

APPENDIX F
MOVIES TO WATCH

2D Movies Staged in Depth

3D can only enhance the depth that is present in the shot. If a scene has not been staged, designed, or photographed with depth, the 3D will be minimal. These traditional 2D movies took advantage of the depth cues and used them to create the illusion of three-dimensional space on a flat 2D screen. This list is not suggesting that these movies should be made in 3D but the directors, photographers, and designers of these films did take advantage of depth. You may not like some of these films but they are all strong visual examples of staging, designing, and photography in depth. Turn off the sound and watch these movies for their staging, production design, and photography in depth.

2001
Back to the Future I
Ball of Fire
Barton Fink
Children of Men
Citizen Kane
Dr. Strangelove
Grapes of Wrath
Hudsucker Proxy
In Cold Blood
King Kong (2005)
Last Picture Show
Magnificent Ambersons
Men in Black
Miller's Crossing
Oh Brother, Where Art Thou?
Paper Moon
Ronin
Rumble Fish
Saving Private Ryan
Strange Days
Terminator 2
The Apartment
The Big Combo
The Killers (1946)
The Matrix
The Trial
Touch of Evil

GLOSSARY

Accommodation
Another word for focus; the opposite of blurry. Refers to images from the eye or a camera lens.

Active 3D glasses
Glasses with a built-in electronic or mechanical shutter that syncs up with the 3D image on a screen.

Active display
A screen that requires active 3D glasses for viewing.

Anaglyph
A stereo picture that requires glasses with a different colored lens for each eye. The stereoscopic pair is separated for the left and right eye using complimentary colors.

Audience Space
The area between the audience and the Stereoscopic Window. See Personal Space.

Autostereoscopic viewing
A system that allows viewing 3D without special glasses.

Beam splitter
A partially silvered mirror placed between two cameras. The beam splitter, depending on its manufacturing, can reflect and transmit different proportions of light.

Bleeding
The left and right eye images of a stereoscopic pair are not fully separated and each eye sees some of the image intended only for the other eye. See Ghosting.

Blending
A method of reducing the Z-axis subject jump between edited shots.

Bokeh
The way a lens renders the out-of-focus quality of objects that are blurred.

Cardboarding
Objects in a 3D movie with so little volume that the object appears to be made of flat cardboard.

Convergence
The inward turning of the eyes to look at an object and bring its image to the same area of the retina in both eyes. We converge when reading a book.

Conversion
A postproduction process by which a 2D movie is transformed to 3D.

Cross-talk
The left and right eye images of a stereoscopic pair are not fully separated and each eye sees the image intended only for the other eye. See Bleeding; Ghosting.

Depth bracket
The total 3D depth measured from the closest foreground object to the farthest background object.

Depth cue
A visual arrangement traditionally associated with 2D pictures that emphasizes or creates the illusion of Z-axis depth.

Depth-of-field

The measurement between the closest and farthest objects in a scene that are in acceptably sharp focus.

Disparity

Similar to parallax; the measured distance between two points of view of the same object as seen by a 3D camera or as presented on a screen.

Divergence

The outward turning of the eyes to look at a stereoscopic image pair.

Emergence

3D objects that come off the screen in negative parallax into the personal space.

Fusion

To combine a stereoscopic image pair into a single object with depth.

Ghosting

An object in depth having too much tonal contrast with its background appears as a faint double image because the image pair is visable to both eyes. See Bleeding; Cross-talk.

H. I. T. or Horizontal image translation

Two cameras are mounted parallel to one another to photograph a stereoscopic pair. To compensate for the parallel optical axis of the two lenses, the cameras' image sensors are offset. The images can also be offset in postproduction.

IO

Interoccular distance: the measured distance between the two pupils of a person's eyes, about 2.5 inches or 63.5 mm.

IA

Interaxial distance: the measured distance between the optical centers of the two lenses on a stereoscopic camera system. This distance is variable on most stereoscopic camera rigs.

Image fusion

To combine a stereoscopic image pair into a single object seen in depth. See Fusion.

Image pair

The left and right eye image that the brain combines into a single three-dimensional image.

Native 3D

A production that was shot using 3D cameras and not converted from a single 2D image.

Occlusion

Overlap; when one object covers part of another object. Sometimes used to describe window violations when only one eye sees a stereoscopic image pair.

Off-screen

Objects that "come off the screen" into the personal space towards the audience like spears, arms etc. that exploit the 3D "poke-in-the-audience's-eye" gag.

Ortho stereoscopic or orthostereoscopic

A type of 3D where the image is photographed and projected life-size to mimic real life.

Over/thru camera arrangement

Two cameras arranged above and behind a beam splitter for 3D photography.

Parallax
The measured distance between two points of view of the same object as seen by a 3D camera or as presented on a screen.

Passive 3D glasses
Glasses with lenses made of a polarized or other light filtering material. These glasses do not have any electronic or mechanical moving parts.

Passive display
A screen that requires passive glasses for 3D viewing.

Personal Space
The area of the theatre between the viewer and the window or Stereoscopic Window.

Polarizer
A glass or plastic filter that organizes light rays.

Rectify
Aligning 3D camera pairs so the camera images are matched in a manner that will permit proper fusion.

Retinal rivalry
Non-fusion of the stereoscopic pair due to improper differences in the image pair.

Rotoscoping
A postproduction technique of tracing the outline of an object for the purpose of extracting that object from a shot. Also used in animation to trace live action objects used as animation reference.

S. I. P or **Stereo image processor**
A trade name registered to 3ality Technica for an electronic device used to evaluate parallax and other functions related to 3D cinematography.

Stereo fusion
A stereoscopic image pair is viewed and combined by the brain into an object that appears in depth. See Fusion.

Stereoscopic image pair
The left and right eye image that the brain combines into a single image seen in depth. See Image fusion; Fusion.

Stereoscopic Window
The masking surrounding a 3D stereoscopic picture that is added in postproduction. This window can be set at the screen plane or moved closer and farther from the audience.

Toe-In
A pair of cameras angle inwards to photograph a stereoscopic pair.

Under/over cameras
Two cameras arranged on either side of a beam splitter for 3D photography.

Under/thru camera arrangement
Two cameras are arranged below and behind a beam splitter for 3D photography.

Vergence
The outward (divergence) or inward (convergence) turning of the eyes to look at an object.

Volume
The amount of apparent three-dimensionality in an object.

Window
The immobile black fabric, plastic, or metal that surrounds a screen. See Stereoscopic Window.

World Space

The area behind the window or Stereoscopic Window.

X-axis

The two-dimensional left-right or horizontal direction of movement or position of objects.

Y-axis

The two-dimensional up-down or vertical direction of movement or position of objects.

Z-axis

The three-dimensional depth direction of movement or position of objects toward or away from the camera or viewer.

ZPS: zero parallax setting

A fully overlapped stereoscopic pair. The two images of the stereoscopic pair are superimposed so it appears to be only a single image. No measurable parallax separation of the stereoscopic image pair.

INDEX

Locators in **bold** refer to figures and tables 2D/3D are filed under two/three-dimensional.